Using Dollars and Sense

John Hannah

Que Corporation
Indianapolis, Indiana

Using Dollars and Sense.

Library of Congress Catalog No.: 85-62359
ISBN 0-88022-164-X

89 88 87 8 7 6 5

Interpretation of the printing code: the rightmost double-digit number is the year of the book's printing; the rightmost single-digit number, the number of the book's printing. For example, a printing code of 83-4 shows that the fourth printing of the book occurred in 1983.

Que Corporation wishes to express its appreciation for Monogram's contribution to the development of this book.

Dedication

This book is for Maureen and Tegan.

Editorial Director
David F. Noble, Ph.D.

Editors
Gregory Croy
Ann Holcombe
Gail S. Burlakoff

Technical Editors
S. E. Cavanaugh
Mark Kalinsky

About the Author

John Hannah

Born in Scotland, John Hannah graduated from the University of East Anglia with a degree in zoology. He worked as a reporter and editor at various newspapers in London before moving to California where he has been a free-lance writer and photojournalist for 10 years. Magazines and newspapers have published hundreds of his articles and photographs, and he has written books on such diverse topics as ocean wildlife, Field Marshall Montgomery, and computer programs.

Composed by Que Corporation
in Garamond

Cover designed by
Listenberger Design Associates

Introduction

1 Basic Dollars and Sense

2 Customizing Dollars and Sense

6 Dollars and Sense and Taxes

7 Business Applications for Dollars and Sense

8 A Lifetime of Dollars and Sense

Appendix A

Appendix B

Appendix C

Appendix D

Appendix E

Acknowledgments

Thank you N.R. and the Monday Night Group for emotional support.

For technical support, special thanks to Sherry Reckas, Jane Gilliam, and all the helpful geniuses at Monogram.

Trademark Acknowledgments

Que Corporation has made every attempt to supply trademarks about company names, products, and services mentioned in this book. Trademarks indicated above were derived from various sources. Que Corporation cannot attest to the accuracy of this information.

Apple is a registered trademark of Apple Computer, Inc.
COMPAQ is a trademark of COMPAQ Computer Corporation.
Dollars and Sense is a trademark of Monogram.
EPSON is a registered trademark of Epson Corporation.
FORECAST is a trademark of Monogram.
Gemini is a trademark of Star Micronics, Inc.
IBM is a registered trademark of International Business Machines Corporation.
IDS is a trademark of Milford Null Modem, Inc.
Macintosh is a trademark licensed to Apple Computers, Inc.
NEC is a registered trademark of NEC Home Electronics (U.S.A) Inc.
OKIDATA is a trademark of Oki America.
TI is a trademark of Texas Instruments, Inc.

Introduction

Money: How Much Is Enough?

What comes to mind when you hear the word *money?* Most of us have the same reaction: "If only I had more of it!"

You probably believe, based on years of struggling and juggling to make ends meet, that this is a reasonable response. But think back to when you were a kid. Remember how your weekly allowance never seemed to go far enough? Today you may earn $20,000, $40,000, or even $80,000 a year, but in all likelihood your current salary does not go far enough either. Perhaps you have discovered this variation of Parkinson's law: "Lifestyles change to exceed any increase in income."

"Never having enough money" is, in most cases, more an attitude than a problem. The real source of distress often is not a shortage of money but a failure to manage your finances effectively. If you work hard for your money, you need to make your money work hard for you.

People fail to take control of their money for various reasons. Many of us put balancing the checkbook on a par with root canal work. Money management at any level can be hard work that takes time and concentration. Managing money is also more complex than ever. Today's average consumer needs a high level of financial sophistication simply to open the right bank account, given the variety of bank accounts available and the differences between them. We have more money, more ways to spend it, and more ways to lose it (as a quick scan of the Tax Code will confirm). Fortunately, technology has provided the personal computer as a way to avoid most of the drudgery.

"Powerful and easy to use" has become a cliche in writing about computers, but applied to Dollars and Sense™, the phrase fits. This program can store all your records for the rest of your life. With Dollars and Sense, you can easily enter and retrieve information. Whenever the need arises, you can print out a report on almost any aspect of your finances. The only complexities that can arise as you use Dollars and Sense are those complexities inherent in your financial strategies.

This book presents Dollars and Sense in the context of good money management and focuses on three main areas: personal finances, tax reporting, and business applications. The personal finances section, which covers in detail such basic information as transaction entry, reporting, graph generation, and other techniques, provides the working knowledge you will need to benefit fully from the other sections.

Computerphobia Is Curable

Computerphobia may not be a real word, but the fear of computers is real. Although there may be millions of personal computers in living rooms, dens, and offices around the world, these machines are, to many of us, suspicious alien objects. A common fear is that using a computer requires high intelligence. This fear is unfounded. In fact, using a computer often seems to increase the user's intelligence. By performing complex and laborious tasks for you at high speed and with utmost efficiency, a computer frees your mind for more creative work.

The way information is stored may also make people uneasy about computers. Most of the methods used (such as tapes, floppy disks, and hard disks) have one thing in common: they are thin magnetized layers that are both "written on" and "read" electronically. The Dollars and Sense program and accounts are stored either on floppy disks or on the Macintosh™ hard-shell version of a floppy disk.

Disks must be handled with care. Do not let the disk's plastic cover get wet, dirty, or greasy. Never touch the exposed part of the inner disk and use only a felt-tip pen to label disks. Keep your disks in a clean, dry, crushproof box away from extreme heat and cold.

Be sure to keep disks away from magnetic fields. Do not set disks near a telephone. Keep disks far from electric motors such as those in vacuum cleaners, fans, and your computer printer. Watch out for refrigerator magnets, screwdrivers, credit cards, and so forth.

If you are careless with your disks, you could lose the entire Dollars and Sense program or destroy the disk's memory of records that you worked on for hours. Accidents are rare but do happen, no matter how careful you are. Therefore, *always make a second, backup copy of each of your disks*. When you finish updating the disk that stores your accounts, copy it. This process of "backing up" a disk should become as natural a habit as breathing.

Take Control of Your Personal Finances

If you have tried to take control of your personal finances before but lost your resolve, keep these hints in mind:

1. Use Dollars and Sense regularly. Half an hour or less a week is enough time to transfer transactions from check register to data base. If you prefer to update your records every few weeks, the sessions will take more time. Bank statement reconciliation and bill paying take about half an hour, once a month.

2. Do not try to do too much too soon. No matter how organized your finances may be, you will probably need several sessions to fit Dollars and Sense to your records and needs. There is no need to impose a harsh regimen on yourself, and no session need be lengthy or rigorous. Unrealistic expectations are a major barrier to financial organization. Many people resolve to get perfect control of their checkbooks, then are so crushed by their first error that they virtually give up. Expect to make mistakes, especially at the beginning. With Dollars and Sense, you can track down mistakes and fix them with little effort, even months after making the errors.

3. Be patient. If buying Dollars and Sense means that you are "turning over a new leaf," do not expect miracles overnight. Nothing is more disconcerting than imagining the completed work. Your project may seem too big, too long term, or too unlikely. Do not let yourself be overwhelmed. Following the scheme of this book, first put your day-to-day money problems in order, then think about larger financial goals.

4. Be persistent. This book tells you all about Dollars and Sense, but will not make you a money expert overnight. Nothing will. But if you are serious about planning a lifetime of good money management, you should investigate every available avenue. Read books on the subject and at least glance daily at your newspaper's

financial pages. Hiring a financial planning consultant, if only for a short time, is also an excellent idea. By using what you learn, you can customize Dollars and Sense to your own situation. Inevitably, a financial planner will ask to see a balance sheet and figures that express your net worth, figures that Dollars and Sense can provide easily.

The Perspective of This Book

Dollars and Sense is a simple program to operate on a variety of computers. Although the perspective of this book is primarily that of the Macintosh user, techniques for other systems are grouped in "Hands-On Hints" sections. Despite differences in appearance, the Macintosh entry windows used as figures in this book have essentially the same function and construction as entry screens on other computers.

1
Basic Dollars and Sense

The Dollars and Sense program develops a data base of the stored records of your financial activity. A data base is an organized body of information or, put another way, a large electronic filing cabinet capable of retrieving any item at high speed. Instead of storing your financial information in ledgers and drawers, Dollars and Sense can store up to 4,000 transactions on each double-sided disk.

Dollars and Sense can also organize your stored information into reports and graphs to help you analyze your financial picture. You will soon discover how your money is allocated, if you can afford a special purchase, what your total income for the year may be, how certain variables may affect your cash flow, what your tax returns will indicate, and so on. Dollars and Sense can help you handle almost any aspect of your finances.

How Dollars and Sense Can Help You

Your Dollars and Sense manual lists a variety of money management tasks that the program can help you accomplish. This book will provide additional information about basic budget management, income tax preparation, profit/loss reports, expense analysis, transferring funds, efficiency comparisons, "what if" forecasts, investment management, credit card management, automatic bill paying, inventories, reconciling bank statements, expense accounting, income statements, balance sheets, cash flow analysis, automatic check writing, and account summaries.

As an electronic bookkeeper and financial planner, Dollars and Sense is a system for entering and recording financial transactions in similar account categories. From these recorded transactions, you can produce the reports, graphs, and predictions essential for good money management decisions. An accountant would recognize Dollars and Sense as a lightning-fast, infallible, and tireless double-entry bookkeeper. A computer buff may guess that all this power and elegance comes from a well-constructed p-System relational data base. But you do not need to be an accountant or a computer expert to see that Dollars and Sense is a simple and reliable way of organizing and controlling your money.

Dollars and Sense Software

Two separate disks are necessary to run your Dollars and Sense program. The program disk included with your Dollars and Sense package holds the actual program itself. The second disk, your "account disk," stores your financial data. The account disk can be a regular 3 1/2-inch or 5 1/4-inch floppy disk or a hard disk. Macintosh owners use the term "files" rather than "disks," but the storage principle is the same.

The Right Hardware

Dollars and Sense is available for the following personal computers:

IBM® PC, PC*jr*™, and PC XT™
Apple® II, II+, IIe, and IIc
Macintosh
Texas Instruments TI PRO

The program can run on many compatible systems. The COMPAQ® personal computer, for example, is fully compatible with the IBM PC and can run the IBM version of the program. If you are unsure of compatibility, your local computer dealer should be able to answer your questions.

Dollars and Sense can operate with the following hardware requirements:

1. Memory. Your system must have at least 64K of memory.
2. Disk Drives. You can run Dollars and Sense on one disk drive, as provided with the IBM PC*jr*, but you will find an extra drive to be a good investment. Using only one drive

requires a certain amount of disk swapping. A message will appear on the screen at intervals asking you to remove the disk in the drive and insert the second disk.

3. Screens and Windows. The most common screen size is 80 columns wide. Some computers, however, use a 40-column "stacked" format; data too long for one line occupies two lines, one above the other. The Macintosh manual refers to screens as "windows." In this book the two terms are interchangeable.

4. The Mouse. The Macintosh and Apple® IIc can be operated with a mouse. You control the movement of the cursor on the screen by rolling the mouse on your desk top or on a special tablet. When the cursor is where you want it, you click a switch on the mouse to select something or initiate some kind of action. To use a mouse with the Apple® IIe, you must have 128K, a mouse card, and the Dollars and Sense program for the Apple IIc.

5. Printer. A printer is useful but not essential. You may want to print your reports and graphs so that you can file "hard copies" for future reference.

Operating Techniques

Whatever the hardware used, Dollars and Sense is a menu-driven program. All program functions are selected and activated through menus or simple lists of available options.

In all systems but the Macintosh, the Main Menu is the starting point for all Dollars and Sense transactions. Menu options are labeled with different letters of the alphabet. You select a particular option by pressing the correct key or moving the cursor to a menu item and clicking the mouse.

Macintosh menus are pulled down from the top of the screen and overlay whatever is being displayed (fig. 1.1). The menu options are highlighted as the cursor passes over them. You select an option by letting up the mouse switch when the right option is highlighted. The menu then rolls back up so that you can proceed with the program. By selecting and activating a menu option, you either get another menu requiring additional information or the entry window.

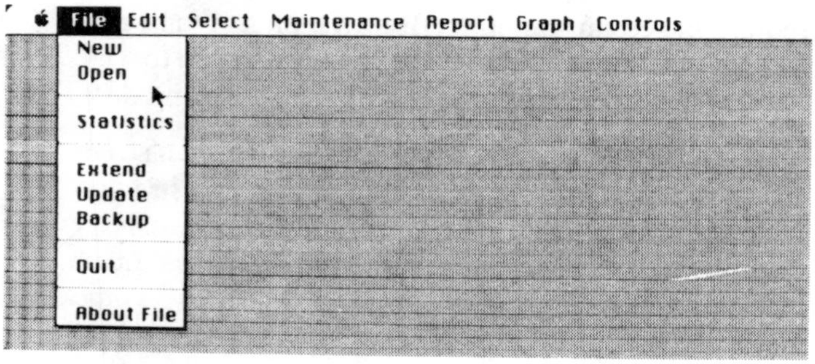

Fig. 1.1. The Macintosh menu system.

On a Macintosh system, you use the entry window as your ledger sheet. With the entry window, you can both enter additional information and ask for a display of your data. The lines you fill out on your entry windows are called "fields" (fig. 1.2).

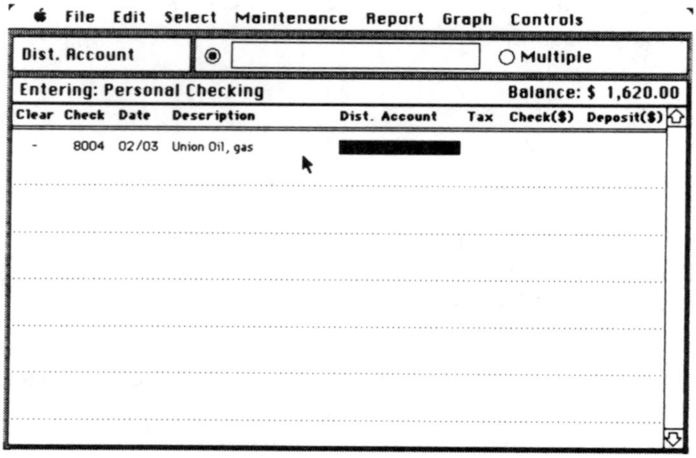

Fig. 1.2. The Macintosh transaction entry window.

Although your computer's screen may appear different from those in this book, the program operates the same way and is equally effective on all systems capable of running Dollars and Sense. As you would expect, the keystrokes for running Dollars and Sense vary from system to system. The differences in screens and operating techniques are most apparent with the Macintosh.

The Dollars and Sense program has a number of features to help you enter data. For example, when you enter an account name, you need not type the name in full. Just type the first two or three letters and press either Return, Enter, or tab, according to your system, for Dollars and Sense to find the complete name. If you find the wrong account, press the equivalent of the horizontal arrow keys to find the account you want. The arrow keys can help you "scroll," or display successive account names in alphabetical order. The right-arrow key scrolls forward through the alphabet; the left-arrow key scrolls backward.

Getting Started for the First Time

Before you start to use Dollars and Sense, make sure the program has been adapted to work with your particular computer. The Macintosh needs no initial adjustment, and Macintosh owners may proceed to Chapter 2, "Customizing Dollars and Sense." If you own a different system, however, and are new to Dollars and Sense, please consult your manual or turn to Appendix A: "Configuring the System" for a discussion of first-time techniques.

Up and Running—Chapter by Chapter

By now you should have a feeling for the scope and organization of Dollars and Sense. You are ready to learn more of how the program works to manage your money, using the techniques described in the remainder of this book. Although practical techniques are emphasized, you will learn some of the concepts behind the techniques. With the assistance of the Dollars and Sense program, you can approach your own financial management in several ways. The theories discussed in this book will help you choose your approach.

Chapter 2 provides information on how to adapt Dollars and Sense to fit your own personal needs. The chapter includes a discussion on the various account types, how to prepare an account file, how to choose a set of accounts, and how to set up budgets for your various accounts.

Chapter 3 discusses the uses of Dollars and Sense that you will ordinarily encounter during the weekly session. You will learn about the base account and how to make transaction entries. The techniques for check distributions and deposit distributions are discussed, followed by explanations and examples of multiple distributions. Some more advanced types of transactions are explained along with using transaction reports to get instant feedback.

Chapter 4 provides explanations for the kind of activities you will use during monthly sessions. The chapter tells how to pay bills automatically using Dollars and Sense and how to set up your printer to print the checks. The techniques for streamlining bank statement reconciliation are presented in detail. More detail is given to budget control including the techniques for doing budget comparison with a composite graph.

Chapter 5 covers the annual session and the financial applications you are likely to encounter in this session. This chapter provides much information on generating the graphs and charts you will need for year-end information including balance sheets, income statements, and net worth. There is even a graph that will plot the trend of your net worth based on financial information in your Dollars and Sense accounts. By the time you reach this point, you will have the tools for setting up your own personal money management system.

Chapter 6 tells you how to keep tax records and generate tax information with Dollars and Sense. This chapter shows you how to produce the figures you will need to fill out your tax forms. Information on how to plan for estimated tax is also presented.

Chapter 7 provides a thorough discussion of the business applications for Dollars and Sense. The chapter includes general information on how to set up your Dollars and Sense business files. With the information provided in this chapter, you can keep accurate financial records of all your business transactions. Specific examples are given for a variety of business situations, examples that you can easily adapt to your own special business needs.

Once you have booted the program and collected your most recent checkbooks, receipts, and other records of your financial activity, you can begin to use Dollars and Sense in earnest. Whether money has always baffled you or you are a seasoned fiscal planner wanting to speed your calculations, Dollars and Sense can bring new ease and clarity to your own money management.

2
Customizing Dollars and Sense

Whether you use Dollars and Sense in business or home management, the program is flexible enough to adjust to your individual record keeping, planning, and reporting needs. Naturally, you will want to personalize your program to reflect your own financial picture.

You can customize your Dollars and Sense program with your own financial information by following these steps:

1. Establish a set of Accounts in a file.
2. Add Accounts, budgets, and starting balances as needed.
3. Give all CHECK Accounts identifying names.
4. Enter and edit transactions.
5. Review progress, using reports of your transactions.
6. Adjust your Accounts and budgets to set your own financial goals.

This chapter deals with the first three steps. You will find guidelines for entering and editing transactions in Chapter 3 along with many examples.

Transactions and Accounts

In accounting, a transaction is any financial event that affects the balance of an account (fig. 2.1). You are making a transaction whenever you pay a bill or deposit a paycheck. The Dollars and Sense program helps you keep track of all your financial transactions.

Check	Date	Description	Dist. Account	Check($)	Deposit($)
8001	02/03	Ace Hardware	Household	25.00	
8002	02/03	Midtown Market	Groceries	125.00	
Deposit	02/03	State Tax Refund	Gross Income		50.00

Fig. 2.1. A transaction affecting another Account.

Dollars and Sense stores records of your transactions in an interrelated collection of accounts. You can store account data on floppy or hard disks depending on your personal computer system.

Account has a special meaning in Dollars and Sense. Most Dollars and Sense Accounts are categories of your own choosing, named for the transactions they record (fig. 2.2). For example, you would record your purchase of a pair of shoes or a shirt in an Account called "Clothing," and the cost of groceries in your "Food" Account.

Please note that in this book when the word *account* refers to a Dollars and Sense Account, the word is capitalized. Otherwise, *account* will not be capitalized. For Dollars and Sense Account types (CHECK, LIABILITY, ASSET, INCOME and EXPENSE), the entire word is capitalized. Account types are discussed in detail later in this chapter.

Accountants call groupings of transactions in similar categories "nominal" accounts. A nominal "food" account includes not only the cost of your groceries but the cost of your restaurant meals as well. Some Dollars and Sense Accounts, however, are not just similar transactions but represent actual bank accounts. These Dollars and Sense, "real" Accounts record all the financial activity, such as checks, deposits, transfers, and so on, that occurs in your bank accounts.

Some Accounts (ASSET, LIABILITY, and CHECKING) have "real," or tangible balances. Other Accounts (INCOME and EXPENSE) do not have tangible balances, but are used for recording purposes. For example, although you could not write a check from your EXPENSE Account, you could write a check from your Checking Account toward an expense.

The categories of accounts that you use every day vary with your individual needs and financial goals. The average American family may have as many as 100 different accounts, such as personal checking, paycheck, groceries, mortgage, mortgage interest, car payments, savings, and so one. (Note that by separating accounts for mortgage and mortgage interest, you can prepare your tax records more easily.)

You can create your own list of Dollars and Sense Accounts to suit your personal needs, or you can begin the program with the set of accounts already provided by Dollars and Sense.

For all the program's sophistication in design, Dollars and Sense uses the centuries-old system of organizing money, "double-entry" bookkeeping. The earliest known double-entry ledgers were kept in Genoa in 1340, although the system was probably in use long before then. Generally accepted as the most reliable way to track money, double-entry bookkeeping clearly shows that every transaction affects at least two accounts, debiting one and crediting another. Duplicating records through this check-and-balance system ensures that any errors will be easy to find.

As an example of how the system works, imagine that you buy a piece of furniture for $200. You have obviously reduced your personal checking account balance, but you have added the value of your new furniture to your furniture account, a calculation needed for determining your financial worth. The $200 that left your personal checking account increases the balance of your furniture account in the same amount.

Sometimes a single transaction affects more than two accounts. Suppose that you are buying your weekly groceries at the supermarket, and you decide that you also need some extra cash. Your food costs $100; you write a check for $125, and the cashier hands you $25 in cash. In this transaction, you have affected three separate accounts.

1. Your personal checking account is reduced by $125.
2. Your groceries account is increased by $100.
3. Your cash account, the amount of cash you have on hand, is increased by $25.

If you were keeping your books the old-fashioned way, you would first record the $125 transaction in a daily journal describing to whom the check was written and why. Then you would record the same transaction in three separate locations in your general ledger.

Dollars and Sense uses a similar process but requires much less effort. You would record the amount of your personal check in the Personal Checking Account and then determine which other Accounts are involved. The program will find the Cash and Groceries Accounts quickly and update them (fig. 2.2).

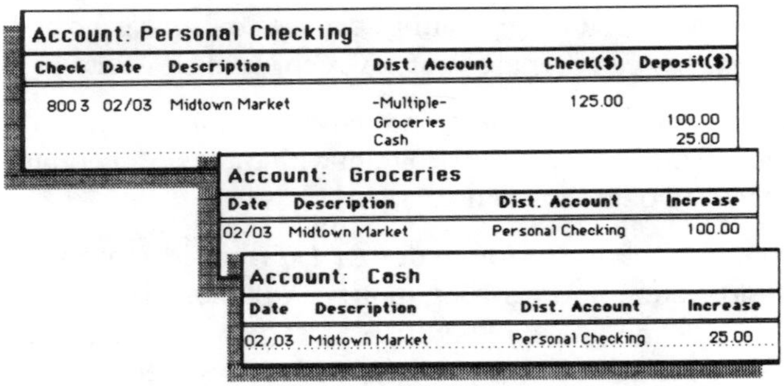

Account: Personal Checking

Check	Date	Description	Dist. Account	Check($)	Deposit($)
8003	02/03	Midtown Market	-Multiple-	125.00	
			Groceries		100.00
			Cash		25.00

Account: Groceries

Date	Description	Dist. Account	Increase
02/03	Midtown Market	Personal Checking	100.00

Account: Cash

Date	Description	Dist. Account	Increase
02/03	Midtown Market	Personal Checking	25.00

Fig. 2.2. A transaction affecting two other Accounts.

Account Types: CHECK, LIABILITY, ASSET, INCOME, EXPENSE

The many varieties of Accounts you will use can be grouped into five different *types:* CHECK, LIABILITY, ASSET, INCOME, and EXPENSE (fig. 2.3).

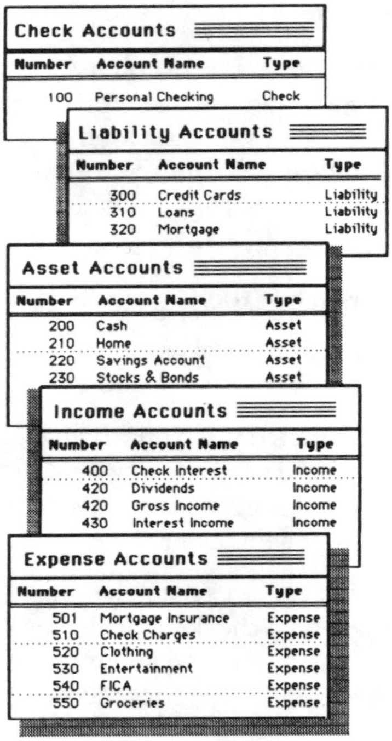

Check Accounts

Number	Account Name	Type
100	Personal Checking	Check

Liability Accounts

Number	Account Name	Type
300	Credit Cards	Liability
310	Loans	Liability
320	Mortgage	Liability

Asset Accounts

Number	Account Name	Type
200	Cash	Asset
210	Home	Asset
220	Savings Account	Asset
230	Stocks & Bonds	Asset

Income Accounts

Number	Account Name	Type
400	Check Interest	Income
420	Dividends	Income
420	Gross Income	Income
430	Interest Income	Income

Expense Accounts

Number	Account Name	Type
501	Mortgage Insurance	Expense
510	Check Charges	Expense
520	Clothing	Expense
530	Entertainment	Expense
540	FICA	Expense
550	Groceries	Expense

Fig. 2.3. The five types of Dollars and Sense Accounts.

Your Personal Checking Account represents a real bank checking account. When you write a check for groceries, you take the value of the check out of the account; you add value with the deposit of your paycheck. You enter these transactions into the type of Dollars and Sense Account called a CHECK Account.

Your LIABILITY Accounts represent the value of what you owe, such as mortgages, loans, or your credit card balance. Because a LIABILITY Account represents a negative value of money, you reduce the balance of a LIABILITY Account when you put money into the Account. If you owe $100 to your bank credit card Account and send a $50 payment, you have reduced your liability. In Dollars and Sense, any transaction that reduces the balance of a LIABILITY Account is called a "payment." Any transaction that increases a LIABILITY Account is a "purchase."

The Cash Account is an ASSET Account. "Asset" is a term applied to anything of value that is owned. The balance of an ASSET Account can be increased or decreased. When you convert part of your supermarket check into cash, you increase your Cash ASSET Account. If you spend $20 on dinner, you will decrease your Cash ASSET Account.

INCOME Accounts record the source of your money. The sources may include salary, dividends, interest, sale of property, and so on.

Your groceries purchase is an example of an EXPENSE Account. EXPENSE Accounts record where your money goes. The $100 you spent at the supermarket increases the balance of this Account.

All these familiar terms have specific meanings in the Dollars and Sense program, so make sure that all your Accounts have been labeled as the correct type. The Account types will be reexamined in the discussion of transaction entry.

Battling the Budget

All Dollars and Sense Accounts can be assigned budgets so that you can pace your financial transactions. Budgets let you have better control of possible surpluses, sudden windfalls, or monetary dangers.

Good budgeting ensures better control of your financial affairs and need not be painful. If you discover that your new budget is difficult to live within, the budget is probably too stringent and requires some additional planning. Think of good budgeting as your tool for establishing financial stability and eventual gain.

The Dollars and Sense program helps you carry out your budget by automating such regular transactions as mortgage payments and paycheck deposits. The "automatic transaction" feature eases your entry of data on the system. You enter these constant amounts only once; the figures can be stored and reactivated when they reoccur. You need to change only the date; the rest is done for you.

Making Financial Predictions

Accountants measure the health of a business or make predictions by relying on a variety of financial statements. You can now base your financial decisions on facts from income statements, balance sheets, cash flow analyses, and so on. To help you make your own financial predictions, your Dollars and Sense program can produce seven different kinds of reports and six types of graphs from the data you have entered.

Some measure of "what if" inquiry is essential to good financial planning. Dollars and Sense gives you the freedom to speculate. For example, you can experimentally change a budget or an income item to see its immediate effect on your total annual budget. Similarly, creating or changing a transaction has an immediate effect on an Account balance.

Preparing an Account File

Your Dollars and Sense records should be stored on disks reserved for the program and your Accounts. If you use the larger-capacity hard disk, your records can be stored with other programs and files. Many hard disk users, however, install the Dollars and Sense program on hard disk but use floppy disks to store Accounts.

After you have set up your program, your next step is to prepare a disk or a Macintosh file for storing your Accounts. To start a file, select "New" from the File Menu. This displays a dialog box for naming and dating the new file and giving the file a set of initial Accounts (fig. 2.4). On other systems, you create a file from a menu called "Begin New Account Disk" or "Start Account Disk."

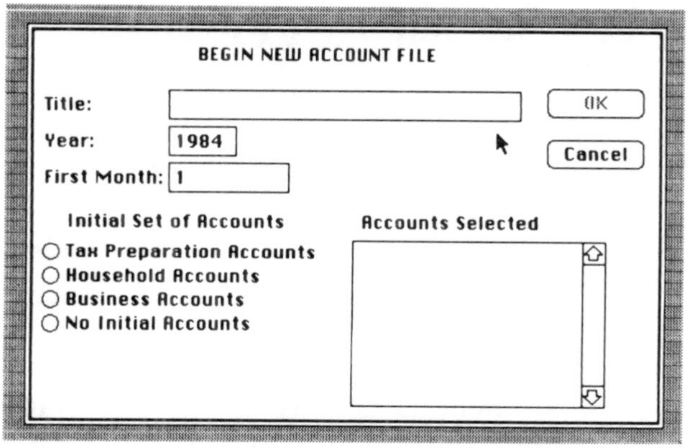

Fig. 2.4. The new account file dialog box.

The Account File Name

Whatever your hardware, give each Account file a title and a beginning date—month and year. You can name a file according to how you use Dollars and Sense. Some users, for example, like to keep as many as three sets of Dollars and Sense "books," one for household accounts, another for tax records, and still another for business accounts. Your files should reflect these different categories and may be changed later as your needs change. Your title not only identifies the file but also appears at the top of the reports and graphs the program generates.

The Account File Month and Year

A file's beginning month need not be the current month but rather the first month of your fiscal year. The fiscal year can be any 12-month accounting period. If you intend to keep Dollars and Sense primarily for personal finances and tax records, begin your fiscal year on January 1. Dollars and Sense will automatically give you January as the beginning of a financial year, but you are free to change this to another date.

ONCE ESTABLISHED, NEITHER THE FISCAL MONTH NOR YEAR CAN BE CHANGED.

Choosing a Set of Accounts

Before the Account file or disk can be used, the right kind of Accounts must be entered to store your transactions. Everyone's list of Accounts will be different, and your Accounts will change as your financial status changes.

To save you time and help you make decisions, Dollars and Sense provides three ready-made sets of Accounts: Tax Preparation, Household, and Business Accounts. You can easily customize these sets by adding the Accounts you need and deleting others.

If you would rather create your own sets of Accounts, remember that each file can have only one set of up to 120 Accounts with 12 CHECK Accounts in each set.

To familiarize yourself with the ready-made accounts, refer to the lists in Appendix D.

1. Household Accounts. The household set of 27 Accounts can be a foundation for your personal financial management system. This set contains the common denominators of almost every financial plan.
2. Business Accounts. The 49 business Accounts can form a template for any client-, product-, or service-based business.
3. Tax Preparation Accounts. Although not intended as a complete tax preparation program, Dollars and Sense can provide all the financial information you need at tax time. You can either incorporate tax-related transactions into your business or personal record keeping, or you can set up a disk reserved solely for taxes. The ready-made set of tax preparation Accounts provides all relevant categories of income and expenditures.

When you make your choice of Accounts, confirm the set by transferring it to your new file (fig. 2.5). Imagine that you have placed empty but correctly labeled folders into an electronic filing cabinet.

Clicking OK in the Macintosh dialog box displays a new box for confirming the new file name and specifying which disk on a two-drive system will store the file (fig. 2.6).

The Main Menu appears after an Account disk has been created on any system but the Macintosh. You can then take Option A to examine your new Accounts and adjust them to suit your needs.

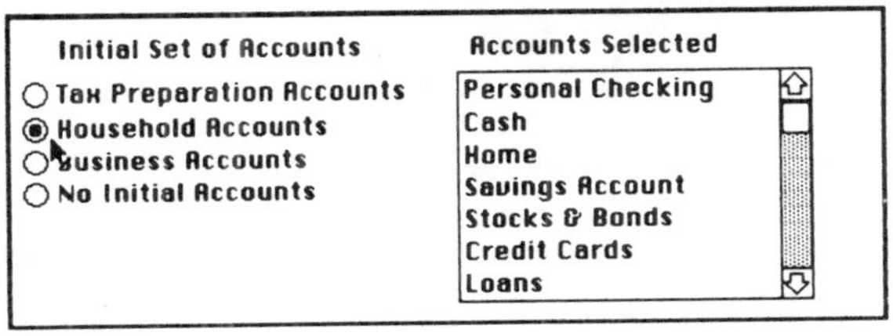

Fig. 2.5. Selecting an Account set.

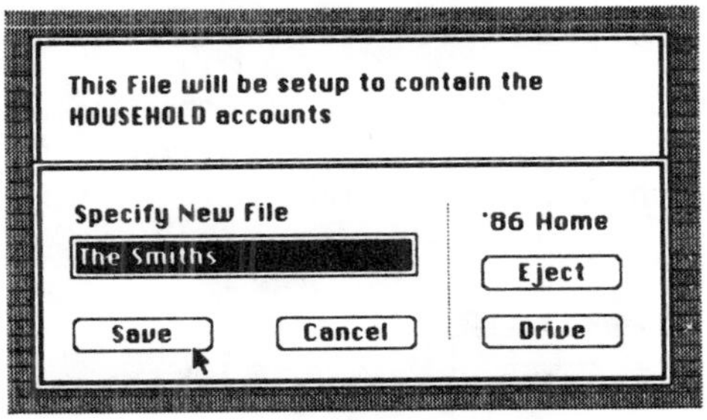

Fig. 2.6. Confirming the name and location of the new file.

The Macintosh screen will remain blank after the name and location of the file are confirmed. The file has indeed been created and can be opened by choosing the second option in the File Menu (fig. 2.7).

Before the file is opened, Macintosh lets you confirm (or select, if you have more than one) which file to open (fig. 2.8).

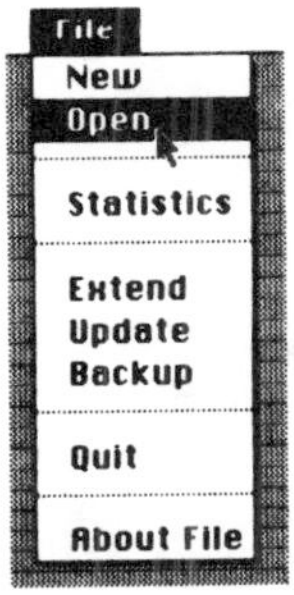

Fig. 2.7. Open *opens the newly-created file.*

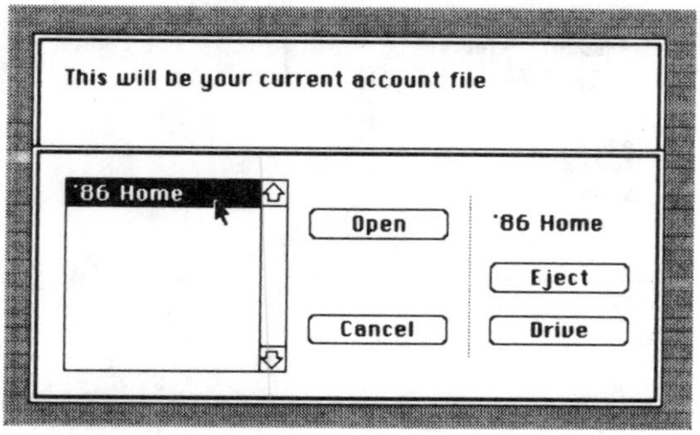

Fig. 2.8. The current file dialog box.

Opening a Macintosh Dollars and Sense file displays figures concerning the information on the file (fig. 2.9). After you have used a file for a while, these figures let you know how much unused space remains in the file.

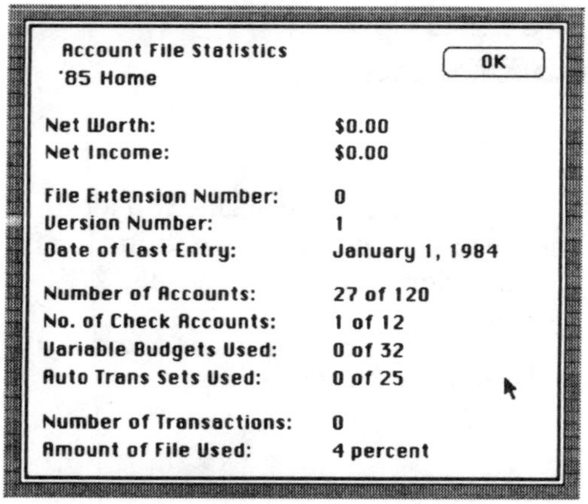

Fig. 2.9. The Account disk statistics.

Displaying the Accounts

When you OK the Macintosh statistics, the screen goes blank. Although no message appears, the file is open; and all menus are operative. You can examine the Accounts by pulling down the Select Menu and choosing Account Definitions (fig. 2.10).

The new Accounts are displayed in a special window, known as the Account definitions window or screen (fig. 2.11) where the Accounts can be modified to suit your needs.

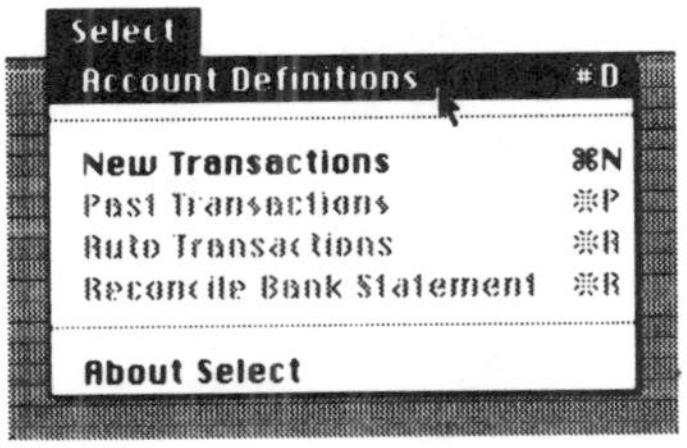

Fig. 2.10. The Select Menu.

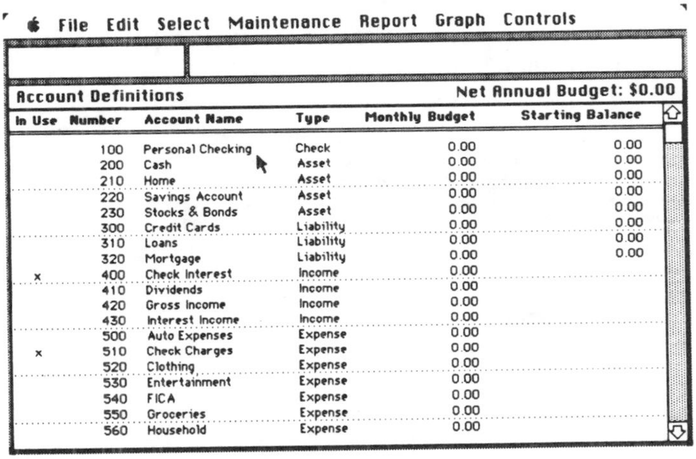
File Edit Select Maintenance Report Graph Controls
Account Definitions
Net Annual Budget: $0.00
In Use Number Account Name Type Monthly Budget Starting Balance
100 Personal Checking Check 0.00 0.00
200 Cash Asset 0.00 0.00
210 Home Asset 0.00 0.00
220 Savings Account Asset 0.00 0.00
230 Stocks & Bonds Asset 0.00 0.00
300 Credit Cards Liability 0.00 0.00
310 Loans Liability 0.00 0.00
320 Mortgage Liability 0.00 0.00
x 400 Check Interest Income 0.00
410 Dividends Income 0.00
420 Gross Income Income 0.00
430 Interest Income Income 0.00
500 Auto Expenses Expense 0.00
x 510 Check Charges Expense 0.00
520 Clothing Expense 0.00
530 Entertainment Expense 0.00
540 FICA Expense 0.00
550 Groceries Expense 0.00
560 Household Expense 0.00

Fig. 2.11. The Account definitions window.

Creating Your Own List of Accounts

Instead of accepting ready-made Accounts, you can define a set of Accounts suited to your own individual needs. When you specify that you want to create your own list, the Account definitions window that appears is not entirely blank, but already contains two mandatory Accounts, `Check Charges` and `Check Interest`, that are necessary for the program to work (fig. 2.12.). The `X` at extreme left indicates that these Accounts are `In Use` and cannot be removed.

An Account needs a number, a name, and a type. A budget and starting balance can also be included. These items of information together make up an Account "definition" that occupies a single line of the screen. Types, budgets, and balances can have an important effect on financial planning and are discussed in more detail later in the book.

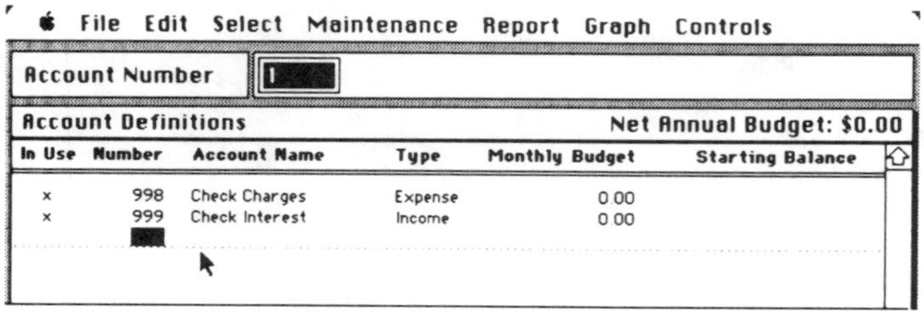

Fig. 2.12. Two check-related Accounts supplied by the program.

To create your own account list with Macintosh, you type the details into the entry box above the screen (fig. 2.13). Pressing tab or Return transfers the information to the definition field.

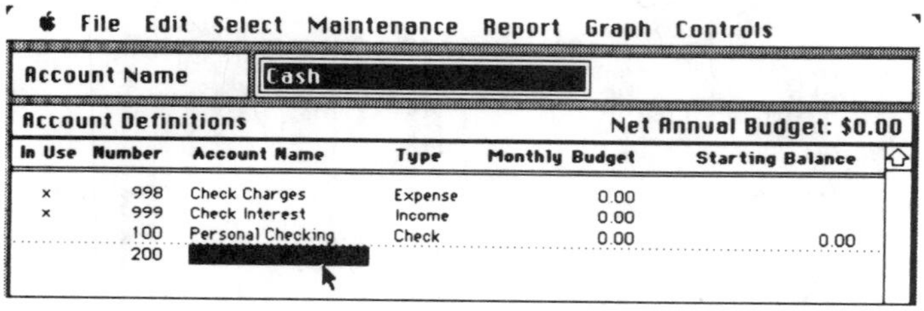

Fig. 2.13. Transferring information to the definition field.

Dollars and Sense can help you write the necessary information in the appropriate fields as you create your Accounts. Account numbers, for example, are automatically supplied in sequence. If you wish to assign your own number, Dollars and Sense will give you the next number in the sequence. To select the Account type, you only need to write the first letter of the Account type (or click a button) for Dollars and Sense to supply the complete word.

The program will lead you naturally through the entry sequence. When you confirm an entry with tab, Return, or by clicking the mouse, the next information needed is highlighted. If you make a mistake, you can return to the error and write over it. (Macintosh users can point and click on the errant field; others can use tab, Escape, or arrow keys.)

Use the following guidelines for defining your Accounts:

1. Numbers: Because Dollars and Sense compiles reports by grouping Accounts by number, your reports will be faster to assemble and easier to read. The field for entering the number of your Account can be seen in figure 2.12. On a

Macintosh the Account numbers are typed into the entry box above the screen. Pressing tab or Return, or clicking the mouse transfers them to the Number field.

2. Account Names: Give your Accounts names that represent a money category. The names do not have to be specific. For example, you can include gas and auto repair costs in a general Auto Expenses Account. (Dollars and Sense can easily extract separate categories from one Account.) Give your CHECK Account the name of the bank where the Account is located.

3. Type: Decide if the Account type is CHECK, LIABILITY, ASSET, INCOME, or EXPENSE. CHECK Accounts are usually bank checking Accounts. ASSET Accounts record the things you own, but can be used in other ways. The money you earn is INCOME. LIABILITY is what you owe. EXPENSE is what you spend on things other than LIABILITY.

4. Monthly Budget: You can set up a budget for any Account, but budgets may be more useful with some Accounts than with others.

5. Starting Balance: All Accounts except INCOME and EXPENSE can have starting balances of money you already have on hand, the value of an ASSET when you set up your disk, or the balance of a LIABILITY that has yet to be paid.

Account Definitions

Deciding which Accounts you need requires some time. If you look at your check register for the last few months, you can see where your money has come from and where your money has gone. You will find your check register a valuable tool in the early stages of using Dollars and Sense because the register is probably the most complete record of your recent financial transactions. Other helpful information can come from last year's tax return and, if you really want to be thorough, last year's canceled checks.

You may not get the Account list right the first time, but try to make the list as complete as you can before you begin. Overestimate rather than underestimate. Accounts that you find you never use are easy to eliminate, but you will save time if an Account is ready for transactions when you need the Account.

Keep in mind that you can always change your set of Accounts to reflect your immediate or changing needs. You can easily change your Account definitions or add and delete Accounts.

Changing Account Definitions

You may want to keep some Accounts in the ready-made set, but prefer to change their names, numbers, or types. For example, if you have more than one checking account, *Personal Checking* will not be specific enough for your use. Try defining your separate checking accounts with the names of your banks or the purpose or use of each account. You can replace any term of the definition by typing a new name over the old one. If you are changing the type of an Account, write only the first letter; Dollars and Sense does the rest for you.

Only with the Macintosh can you edit definitions whenever the definitions screen is displayed. You can stop in the middle of creating a new Account and go to an entirely different Account definition that needs changing. On other personal computers, keep in mind that your screen operates in separate edit or enter modes.

Adding New Accounts

New Accounts can be created as your financial needs change. The maximum number of Accounts per file is 120, but this could be more than you will use.

Macintosh users create new Accounts by selecting `Add Line` from the Edit Menu (fig. 2.14).

Saving New Accounts

If you save your newly created Accounts on your Account disk before adding starting balances or budgets, your Dollars and Sense program will arrange all your Accounts in numerical order. You will find it easier to locate Accounts with the numerical arrangement. Macintosh users can save Account definitions by selecting `End Edit` from the Edit Menu (fig. 2.15).

Identifying CHECK Accounts

To avoid any errors in your bank accounts, you will want to make sure your CHECK Accounts cannot be confused. Your CHECK Account

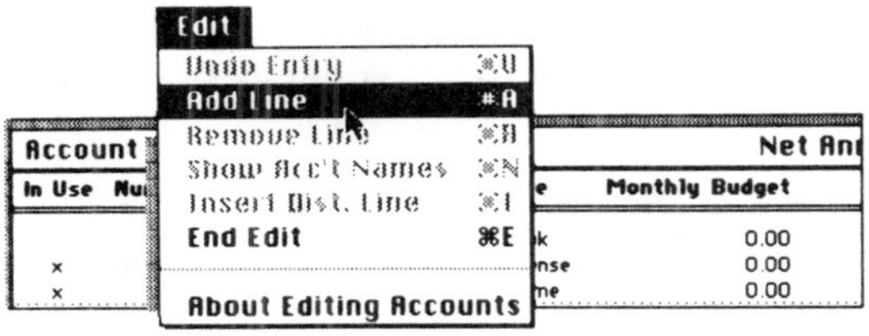

Fig. 2.14. Adding new Accounts.

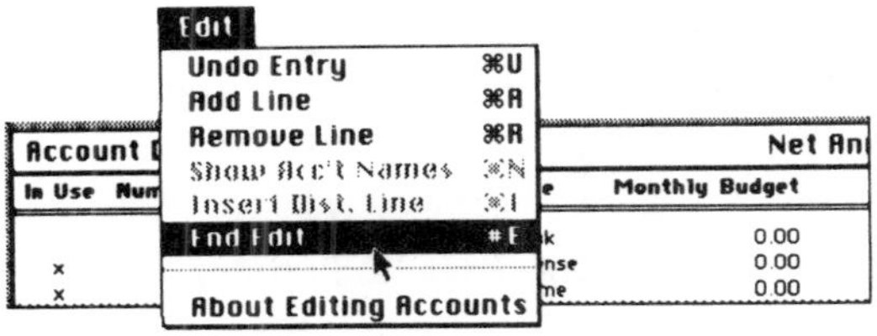

Fig. 2.15. Selecting End Edit *from the Macintosh Edit Menu.*

data window appears automatically when a new CHECK Account is saved (fig. 2.16). Use the menu option to display the CHECK Account data window when you want to change an item.

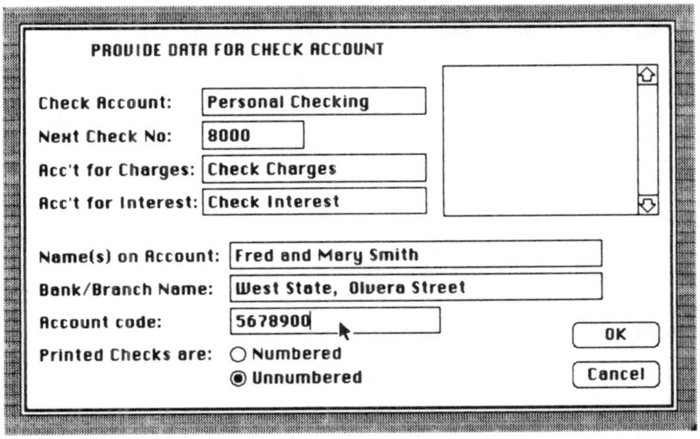

Fig. 2.16. The CHECK Account data window.

With the CHECK Account data window you can confirm or establish the following data for a CHECK Account:

1. The name of the CHECK Account is displayed. If this window appears because a new Account is saved, the new Account's name is displayed here automatically.

2. Check numbers appear in sequence. The next CHECK Account entry screen will display the next number automatically.
3. The names of Accounts reserved for check charges and check interest are already established, but you can change them if you like.
4. The names of the owners of the account are displayed.
5. The bank name and branch are displayed.
6. The account code which appears along the bottom of your checks is displayed. The code is the electronically-readable account number along the bottom of your checks.
7. The choice of numbering your checks on the printer is displayed. Checks can be produced without numbers.

Fixed Accounts

You can easily edit and delete Account numbers, names, types, starting balances, and budgets. Some limitations, however, safeguard your data. To change the Account type or delete an Account, you must first empty the Account of all transactions.

Fixed Accounts and those containing transactions are easily identified on Apple family screens through highlighting. The Macintosh window has an `In Use` column at the extreme left, in which an `X` appears as a signal that the Account cannot be removed from the set.

Starting Balances for Starting Files

Only ASSET, LIABILITY, and CHECK Accounts have starting balances. For an ASSET Account, the starting balance can be the value of the asset when the Account is created. For LIABILITY Accounts, the starting balance is what you owe when you create the Account. For CHECK Accounts, the starting balance is the amount with which you open your Account.

Starting balances can be your basis for record keeping. Ideally, a Dollars and Sense Account file should record financial activity for a complete year, with January 1 as the beginning of the fiscal year. If you start Dollars and Sense later in the year, you need to make your yearly records current.

To make your records current, when you first set up your Dollars and Sense files, enter all your financial activity since January 1, taking the information from your check register and bank statements. You can build up a complete record of your finances for the year, and you can see how you spend your money which will help you set up helpful budgeting.

The alternative is to begin with starting balances only (fig. 2.17). Your records may not be complete enough for your next tax return, but you can ensure more accurate record keeping. Your monthly budgets should be established in the current month as variable budgets, which balance monthly instead of yearly (fig. 2.18). You can set up a maximum of 32 variable budgets. Variable budgets are discussed later in greater detail.

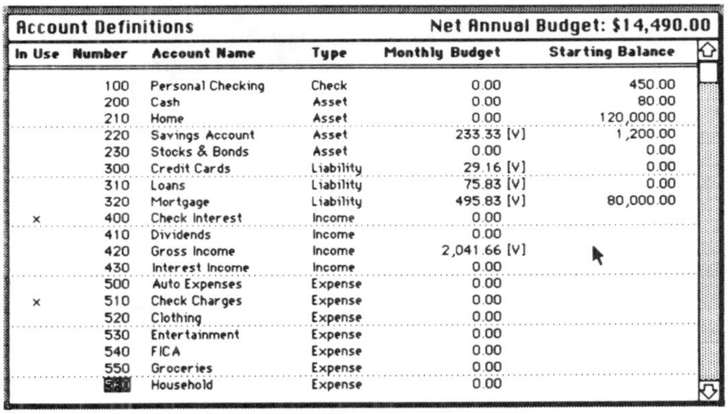

Account Definitions — Net Annual Budget: $14,490.00

In Use	Number	Account Name	Type	Monthly Budget	Starting Balance
	100	Personal Checking	Check	0.00	450.00
	200	Cash	Asset	0.00	80.00
	210	Home	Asset	0.00	120,000.00
	220	Savings Account	Asset	233.33 [V]	1,200.00
	230	Stocks & Bonds	Asset	0.00	0.00
	300	Credit Cards	Liability	29.16 [V]	0.00
	310	Loans	Liability	75.83 [V]	0.00
	320	Mortgage	Liability	495.83 [V]	80,000.00
x	400	Check Interest	Income	0.00	
	410	Dividends	Income	0.00	
	420	Gross Income	Income	2,041.66 [V]	
	430	Interest Income	Income	0.00	
	500	Auto Expenses	Expense	0.00	
x	510	Check Charges	Expense	0.00	
	520	Clothing	Expense	0.00	
	530	Entertainment	Expense	0.00	
	540	FICA	Expense	0.00	
	550	Groceries	Expense	0.00	
	560	Household	Expense	0.00	

Fig. 2.17. Starting balances and budgets.

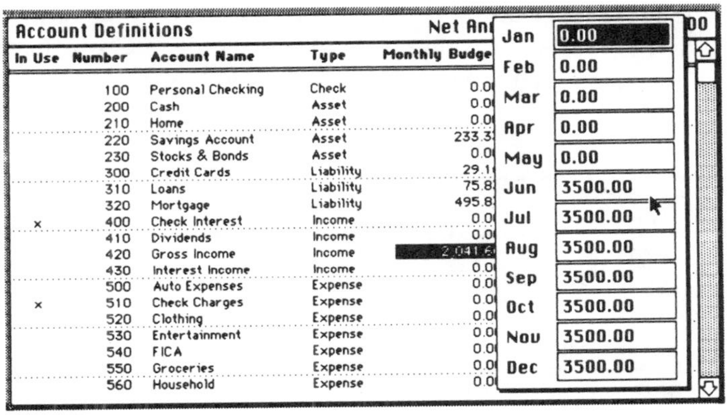

Account Definitions — Net Ann…

In Use	Number	Account Name	Type	Monthly Budge…
	100	Personal Checking	Check	0.0
	200	Cash	Asset	0.0
	210	Home	Asset	0.0
	220	Savings Account	Asset	233.3
	230	Stocks & Bonds	Asset	0.0
	300	Credit Cards	Liability	29.1
	310	Loans	Liability	75.8
	320	Mortgage	Liability	495.8
x	400	Check Interest	Income	0.0
	410	Dividends	Income	0.0
	420	Gross Income	Income	2,041.6
	430	Interest Income	Income	0.0
	500	Auto Expenses	Expense	0.0
x	510	Check Charges	Expense	0.0
	520	Clothing	Expense	0.0
	530	Entertainment	Expense	0.0
	540	FICA	Expense	0.0
	550	Groceries	Expense	0.0
	560	Household	Expense	0.0

Month	Budget
Jan	0.00
Feb	0.00
Mar	0.00
Apr	0.00
May	0.00
Jun	3500.00
Jul	3500.00
Aug	3500.00
Sep	3500.00
Oct	3500.00
Nov	3500.00
Dec	3500.00

Fig. 2.18. Variable INCOME budget used to set up a file in June.

A "Dummy" Account for INCOME and EXPENSE Starting Balances

Data cannot be entered directly into INCOME and EXPENSE Accounts, but is displayed there only through activity in other Accounts. Dollars and Sense therefore does not provide the capacity for giving starting balances to INCOME or EXPENSE Accounts. Starting balances are not usually needed for these Accounts, but as you set up your first Account disk, you may want to show the income you have earned and the expenses you have incurred since January. How will you give INCOME and EXPENSE Accounts starting balances when the Account definitions screen will not let you?

You know that your previous income and expenses show as part of your checkbook and your savings records. You may, however, want to reconstruct an accurate record of these transactions by entering your previously-earned income and expenses into the Accounts.

The solution is to create a "dummy" Account whose sole purpose is to supply starting balances for INCOME and EXPENSE Accounts (fig. 2.19). The dummy Account must begin as an ASSET Account.

Account Definitions

In Use	Number	Account Name	Type	Monthly Budget	Starting Balance
	800	Dummy Balance	Asset	0.00	0.00

Fig. 2.19. Dummy Accounts must begin as an ASSET type.

You can now go into this Account by selecting `New Transactions` and write transactions that transfer the starting balances into your various INCOME and EXPENSE Accounts. For example, suppose you have earned $17,500 since January and spent $500 on auto expenses. Write them in the transactions entry screen as shown in figure 2.20.

Editing: Dummy Balance

Base Account	Date	Description	Dist. Account	Tax	Decrease	Increase
Dummy Balance	06/12	balance	Gross Income	-		15,000.00
Dummy Balance	06/12	balance	Auto Expenses	-	500.00	

Fig. 2.20. Dummy Accounts to be transferred to INCOME and EXPENSE Accounts.

You must be sure to shift the EXPENSE figure to the `Decrease` column. The effect of these entries is to change the balances of the designated

INCOME and EXPENSE Accounts to bring them up to date. Once starting balances have been established, put an undistributed transaction into the dummy Account that reduces its balance to zero. You must never use this Account again. Do not throw the Account away because the loss of the Account would detract from your overall picture, but change the Account's name to something like "Never Use This One."

Budgeting with Dollars and Sense

The subject of budgets is central to any money management system. The word *budget* originally meant a purse and gradually came to mean a plan for spending what was in the purse. Many people think of budgeting as nothing more than a plan for spending money. Dollars and Sense gives you the advantage of being able to apply budgets to any type of Account to create a comprehensive picture that includes not only how much you will spend but also what you expect to earn and own.

The twofold purpose of a budget is to plan and control money. A budget cannot tell you *exactly* what is going to happen, but a budget can tell you *probably* what is going to happen. When a budget has been in operation for some time, you can see how realistic your budget is. Keep in mind that you can always make changes if needed.

Financial health depends on the philosophy, psychology, and techniques of good budgeting. Creating budgets with your Dollars and Sense program is easy. Begin by typing a figure from a transaction into the `Monthly Budget` column. If you foresee that the income or expenditure will change throughout the year, you can enter the item into the corresponding month in the `Variable Budget` column.

Fixed Budgets

Any Account can have a monthly budget. EXPENSE and ASSET Account budgets represent the amount you can afford to spend that month. INCOME budgets show what you expect to earn. LIABILITY budgets are what you must pay. CHECK Account budgets can show the minimum balance that some interest-earning Accounts require.

Variable Budgets

A variable budget is one that reflects different amounts for every month throughout the year. If your work is seasonal or dependent on demand, your income will change from month to month. A liability such as a car loan may be paid off before the year is through (fig. 2.21). A variable budget will handle the monthly changes in these Accounts.

Macintosh users can create a variable budget by clicking the `Variable` indicator when the `Monthly Budget` entry box appears. A ladder of entry boxes appears, one for each month of the year. Put the pointer on a month, click the mouse, and enter the budget. Press the tab key to move to the next month, and press Return to save. In the Account definitions window, variable budgets are indicated by `(V)` following a budget figure. This figure is the average monthly amount of a variable budget.

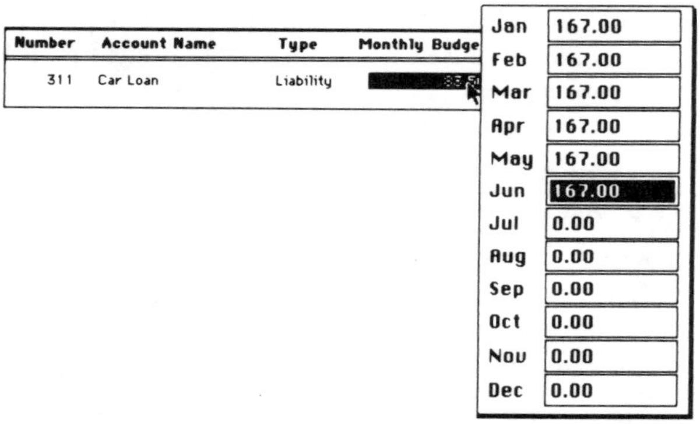

Fig. 2.21. A variable budget for a car loan.

Hands-On Hints

Variable Budgets

You create variable budgets for income or expenditures that vary month by month. Use variable budgets if you are beginning your budget with the current month or if you are setting up your Dollars and Sense program for the first time in any month other than January.

The Apple Family

Use your tab and the up- and down-arrow keys to reach the monthly budget field. Press the V key. The Variable Budget column expands to show all 12 months of the year.

Press Return (or Enter) to get to the right month and enter the amount due. This amount may be repeated for subsequent months when you press Return, but you can type different amounts (such as zero) if you need to. Pressing Return after the December field establishes the variable budget and makes the budget column disappear. The word *variable* in the monthly budget column shows that the amount has been entered for that month. Press the V key for "variable" to examine the budget column.

Net Annual Budget Balance

The net annual budget balance appears at the top right of the Account definitions window (fig. 2.22). This figure changes with every new budget you create and shows how your predicted income compares with your predicted expenses. If the balance is a negative figure, you are planning to spend more than you expect to earn. You can expect a surplus when the balance is positive. Ideally, your balance should be somewhere around zero, which indicates you have planned well how you will use your proposed income.

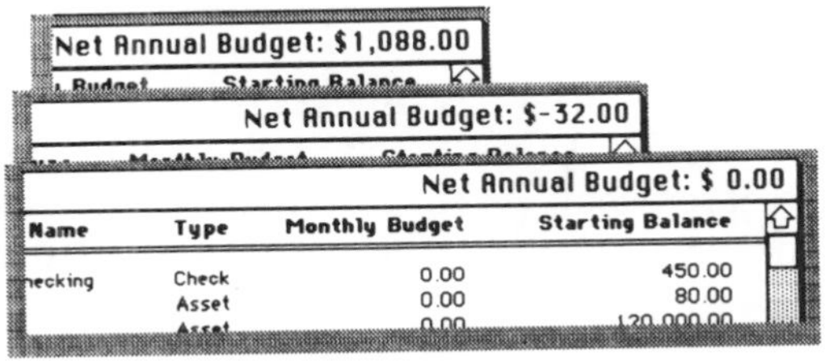

Fig. 2.22. The net annual budget balances.

The net annual budget balance is a useful tool for creating "what if" plans. For example, you could use the budget balance to see if you can afford to repay a contemplated loan. Set up the monthly loan repayment as a budget for your Loans Account (or for an Account created specially for the loan) and see how the net annual budget balance changes. If the result is negative, you can make similar experiments with other expenditures, income, or even asset budgets to find extra money for the loan. Ideas to check out are: reducing your entertainment budget, selling an asset, or finding another source of income.

LIABILITY Budgets

To be successful at budgeting, you should be able to identify the predictable and unpredictable items in your budget. Your financial obligations may be difficult to control but easy to predict. Your mortgage payments are easy to predict but difficult to alter if you cannot afford your monthly payments. Identifying uncontrollable budgets gives you the first fixed points in a constantly changing financial picture.

The least avoidable liabilities are of course the easiest to identify, such as your mortgage or your car loan. Both of these budgets in a sense represent payment schedules. If either of them is due to be paid off this year, you can make them variable budgets.

Credit card liabilities should be considered next. Scheduling credit card repayments demonstrates the flexibility that is an important feature of most budgets. You may decide to budget for the varying minimum monthly repayment, which must be reestablished every month. Alternatively, you can reduce your liability by curbing your credit card purchases and budgeting a rapid repayment schedule.

ASSET Budgets

In managing personal finances, your savings are the first ASSETS you should budget. Economists have varying ideas about how much you should save each year, but most recommend that you try to save at least five percent of your net income in long-term savings, twice that if you are over 45.

After providing for savings, you may want to budget for a more concrete asset, such as an antique collection. The net annual budget balance in the Account definitions window can give you an idea of how much surplus income is available for placing into ASSETS.

INCOME Budgets

Your income can serve as a major fixed item in your budget. If you are a salaried employee, divide your yearly salary by 12 to predict your monthly income. Include the variable items you expect to receive such as a Christmas bonus or stock interest. To predict your net income, estimate withholding tax for the year and budget for the tax in the appropriate EXPENSE Accounts.

If you are self-employed, try to take your clues from the tax returns of the past couple of years. After using your Dollars and Sense program for a while, you should be able to estimate income more confidently with the help of your many new graphs and reports.

EXPENSE Budgets

Because your payouts control your cash flow, good expense budgeting can mean the difference between the success and failure of any management plan. Expense budgets should be simple enough to be understood and easily updated, yet comprehensive enough to include any significant variable in cash flow.

List your personal expenses in the order of size and importance. After your liabilities have been paid, what are your greatest expenses? Your check register, once again, can provide this information. You will find the Dollars and Sense program another good source for analyzing your previous expenses. After a few weeks of using the program, you can call for an "Actuals vs. Budgets" report for an appraisal of your spending patterns. Use the report to fine-tune your budgets.

Remember to include an adjustment in your budget for inflation. Inflation is variable and unpredictable. Use your own judgment based on the current inflation rate, the inflation trend of the past few months, and the predictions of financial experts whose opinions you value.

To sum up, the first law of budgeting is the same as the one written on the wall of the temple at Delphi several thousand years ago: "Know Thyself." Know your needs and goals, your habits and foibles. First and foremost, know exactly where your money is going to and coming from. Dollars and Sense, used wisely, can provide the knowledge.

3
When To Use Dollars and Sense

Think of four types of sessions—occasional, weekly, monthly, and annual—as times to use Dollars and Sense. Use occasional sessions for anything you want to know right away, such as finding out how much you have in an Account, or investigating what would happen if you make a large financial transaction. Weekly sessions, used to enter recent transactions, should take no more than half an hour of your time. Monthly sessions are for paying bills, reconciling your bank account, and checking progress. You need annual sessions to evaluate your net worth, update inventories, and collect tax information. For at least the first few months, you will also need time to fine-tune your budgets and change your strategy if necessary.

Before discussing specific operations, a review of the kinds of Accounts you may need will be useful. The ready-made Household set of Accounts provides a convenient starting place (fig. 3.1).

The CHECK Accounts

Dollars and Sense CHECK Accounts correspond to actual bank accounts and to similar accounts in savings and loan institutions. There can be as many as 12 CHECK Accounts in a file. These Accounts are not just records but control the movement of money. (EXPENSE Accounts, on the other hand, simply keep a record of the amount spent.)

The CHECK label has special significance in Dollars and Sense programming. CHECK Accounts are the most common medium for entering transactions and for distributing records of those transactions

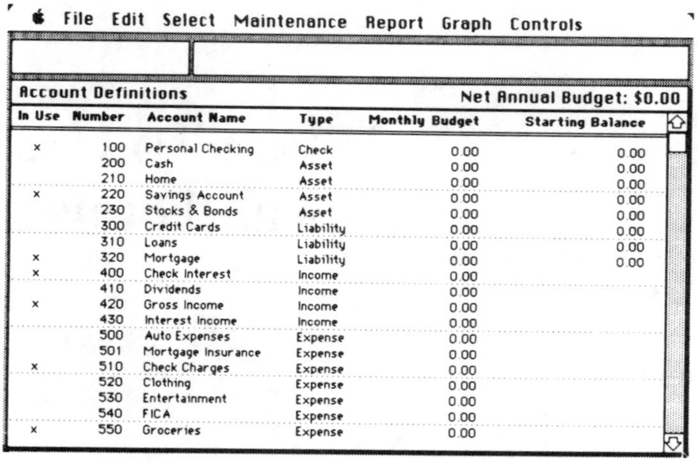

In Use	Number	Account Name	Type	Monthly Budget	Starting Balance
x	100	Personal Checking	Check	0.00	0.00
	200	Cash	Asset	0.00	0.00
	210	Home	Asset	0.00	0.00
x	220	Savings Account	Asset	0.00	0.00
	230	Stocks & Bonds	Asset	0.00	0.00
	300	Credit Cards	Liability	0.00	0.00
	310	Loans	Liability	0.00	0.00
x	320	Mortgage	Liability	0.00	0.00
x	400	Check Interest	Income	0.00	
	410	Dividends	Income	0.00	
x	420	Gross Income	Income	0.00	
	430	Interest Income	Income	0.00	
	500	Auto Expenses	Expense	0.00	
	501	Mortgage Insurance	Expense	0.00	
x	510	Check Charges	Expense	0.00	
	520	Clothing	Expense	0.00	
	530	Entertainment	Expense	0.00	
	540	FICA	Expense	0.00	
x	550	Groceries	Expense	0.00	

Fig. 3.1. The ready-made set of Household Accounts.

to other Accounts. When compiling graphs and reports, Dollars and Sense treats a CHECK Account balance as an ASSET. Savings accounts used to pay bills can become CHECK Accounts.

100 Personal Checking. There is only one CHECK Account in the ready-made list. You will probably want to change the name "Personal Checking" to another that includes the name of your bank to differentiate this Account from other CHECK Accounts that you may add later.

The LIABILITY Accounts

Liabilities are financial obligations such as mortgages, loans, and credit card balances.

300 Credit Cards. Create an Account for each of your credit, charge, and travel and entertainment cards. Whenever you buy something with a credit card, you incur a liability that must be paid back. Credit cards are convenient, but that convenience can be expensive. Credit card control is easy with Dollars and Sense, which helps you see exactly what the cards really cost.

310 Loans. This will be the only Loan Account you need if you have just one outstanding loan in addition to your mortgage. If you have several loans, create an Account for each.

320 Mortgage. Your home may be your greatest asset as well as your greatest liability. When you begin this Account, use the total unpaid amount of your mortgage as the starting balance. This Account always shows what you owe.

The ASSET Accounts

ASSET Accounts usually record the value of such possessions as your house, car, art objects, furniture, and jewelry. Business assets include machinery, equipment, and accounts receivable. To know how much you are worth, keeping close track of your assets is essential.

Special ASSET Accounts can be created for the sole purpose of balancing other Accounts, an important technique discussed in detail later in this chapter.

200 Cash. This Account can record cash on hand.

210 Home. Your home is probably your biggest single asset. Whether or not you own your home outright, you need an ASSET Account that records your home's complete resale value. You can update this Account as the market changes. When you begin this Account, the starting balance is the price paid for your home.

220 Savings. Everyone needs at least one Savings Account. Savings Account names must indicate the name of the bank or savings institution where the accounts are kept. A Savings Account that is used often, especially to pay bills, should be a CHECK Account rather than an ASSET Account.

230 Stocks and Bonds. Use this ASSET Account for your stocks who do like to speculate, Dollars and Sense can help keep records of your holdings. You would, however, need to create several different Accounts for long-term gains, short-term gains, options, brokerage commissions, and so on.

The INCOME Accounts

INCOME Accounts record the source of your money—wages, dividends, interest, royalties, winnings, and so on.

400 Check Interest. The interest earned by checking accounts must be reported as income. Your bank should send you regular statements that show interest earned. The Check

Interest Account, an essential part of the bank statement reconciliation process, is one of two mandatory Accounts in the program. You cannot delete the Account, but you can change the Account's name or number.

410 Dividends. Various types of dividends are considered income and must be reported separately on your tax forms.

420 Gross Income. This Account records (before taxes and deductions) all income distributed to other Accounts. By creating a different Income Account for each wage earner in a two-paycheck (or more) family, you can make tax reporting easier.

430 Interest Income. Record all interest income, other than check interest, separately. Examples of interest income include savings accounts, municipal bonds, money market funds, certificates of deposit, and so forth. The balance of the Account at the end of the year can be transferred to your tax form.

The EXPENSE Accounts

EXPENSE Accounts show where much of your money goes. Information provided by these Accounts can help you manage your money because curbing expenses is often easier than increasing income. Many EXPENSE Account balances are also needed to estimate taxes.

500 Auto Expenses. This Account includes all car expenses (insurance, gas, repairs, and so on). A transaction report can easily extract individual expenses from this Account. You can also create a Business Auto Expenses Account for a vehicle used solely for business.

510 Check Charges. This mandatory Account is used to record charges from checking accounts as those charges appear on your bank statements.

520 Clothing. This Account records what you or your family spend on clothing. If your budget is stringent, create a Clothing Account for each family member and give each person a budget.

530 Entertainment. This Account can track your entertainment expenses and help you budget them. To record business entertainment expenses separately, you can create a special Business Entertainment Account.

540 FICA. This Account keeps a record of your federal insurance contributions throughout the year.

550 Groceries. Keep a record of how much you spend on groceries. This may be a good place to start controlling expenses.

560 Household. Use this Account for recording the miscellaneous expenses of running a household. If many of the expenses are for home improvements, you may want to create a separate Account for those expenses.

570 Loan Interest. Use this Account for interest paid on all loans other than your mortgage (personal loans, credit cards, and so on). Most interest paid is tax-deductible.

580 Medical/Dental. Payments for doctors, dentists, drugs, hospitals, and so on must be recorded in this Account. At tax time, you can split the payments into individual categories.

590 Miscellaneous Expenses. This is a convenient place to record expenses that do not fit anywhere else. You may discover that certain miscellaneous expenses deserve an Account of their own.

600 Mortgage Interest. Mortgage interest can be a large tax deduction, particularly if you bought your home recently.

610 Taxes-Federal. To calculate your taxes accurately, you need to record the federal income tax withheld from your paycheck. Your paycheck stub supplies the figures.

620 Taxes-Property. Use this Account to record property taxes paid. You can set up a variable budget for this Account to remind you when taxes are due.

630 Taxes-State You must record any state and local taxes paid.

640 Utilities. All your utility payments can be recorded in a single Account. For a more convenient, detailed study of utility expenses, create an Account for each.

Occasional Sessions

The weekly, monthly, and annual sessions with Dollars and Sense are regular sessions that are scheduled in advance. The regular sessions are scheduled to provide timely periods of financial planning, recording, bill paying, and so on. Occasional sessions are for immediacy. Use occasional sessions when you want information right away or when you have a bill you want to pay immediately or when you want to see how a purchase you want to make the next day will affect your budget.

You do not have to wait for regular sessions to work with any aspect of your finances. Dollars and Sense is ready when you are. The techniques and procedures you will learn for weekly, monthly, and annual sessions are the same ones you will use in occasional sessions.

Weekly Sessions

For the average Dollars and Sense session, gather up all available records of your recent income and expenses—your check register, credit card statements, paycheck stubs, cash receipts, and so on.

Your most valuable record can be your check register. Kept correctly, the register will show the number, date, payee, and amount of every check, the date and amount of deposits, and the current balance. Make a habit of filling in the register before, not after, you write a check.

After updating your Dollars and Sense records, store the receipts for sums over $25 in a safe place. (An accordion folder with a compartment for each month is an excellent container.) In the event of an audit, the IRS is unlikely to accept your Dollars and Sense records, however accurate, as uncorroborated evidence. The IRS requires either receipts that bear the name of the business, the date, the amount, and the purpose of the transaction, or card-holder copies of credit card purchases.

The Base Account and Transaction Entry

Think of a Base Account as your way into the program. Transactions entered into the Base Account can be distributed to other Accounts, saving you the trouble of accessing each individual Account.

Only CHECK, ASSET, or LIABILITY Accounts can be designated as Base Accounts for transaction entry. Transactions can be entered directly into these Accounts. True Base Accounts are usually payment Accounts, with CHECK Accounts the most commonly used Base Account for everyday money management. ASSET and LIABILITY Accounts used as Base Accounts for specialized functions are discussed later in this book. To appear in an EXPENSE or INCOME Account, the record of a transaction must first be entered into a CHECK, ASSET, or LIABILITY Account.

The Account Selection Menu on all computers except the Macintosh takes different forms for different functions and can create confusion about Base Accounts. For example, when you enter transactions, you use the first option, `[A] Base Account --}`, to specify into which Account the transactions go. In this context, you have a true Base Account. Dollars and Sense will allow you to enter only a CHECK, ASSET, or LIABILITY Account.

Sometimes the Account Selection Menu has a different function. When used to specify an Account for which you want a transaction report, the first option is still `[A] Base Account --}`. In this context, however, the Account is not a true Base Account because Dollars and Sense will allow you to enter any type of Account, including EXPENSE and INCOME.

Using an Account Selection Menu or Macintosh dialog box, you can select a Base Account for transaction entry. The Macintosh box is displayed by clicking `New Transactions` from the Select Menu (fig. 3.2), then clicking the name of the Account you want in the dialog box (fig. 3.3). Only the accessible Accounts (CHECK, LIABILITY, or ASSET) are displayed in the scroll box. The windows for entering transactions vary according to Account type. We will examine these differences as they occur.

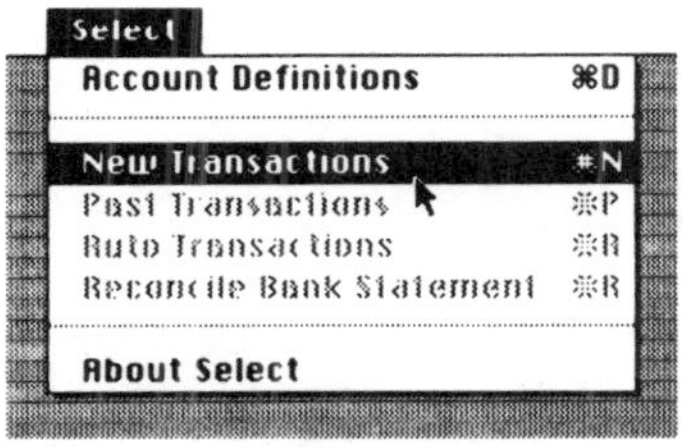

Fig. 3.2. Selecting `New Transactions` *in the Macintosh Select Menu.*

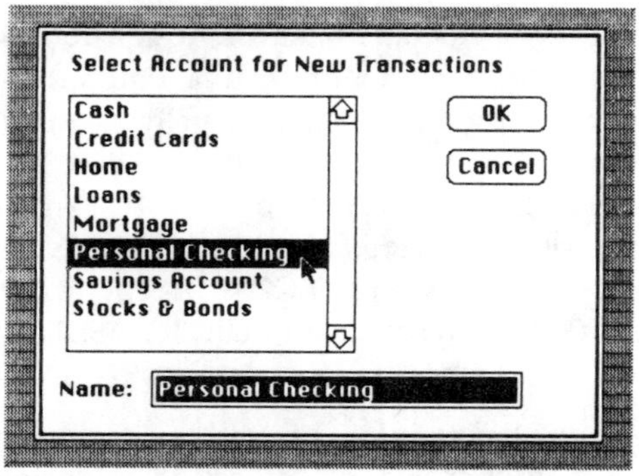

Fig. 3.3. Choosing a Base Account for transaction entry.

Hands-On Hints

Account Selection Menus

The Apple Family

For the Apple II, II+, and IIe, the medium for selecting a Base Account is called the Account Selection Menu. For the IIc, the menu is called Enter Transactions. In essence both menus are the same.

All the menus have options for specifying the Base Account and for setting the current date and the next check number. The name of the Base Account can be found by searching and scrolling, a useful technique that is discussed in detail later in this chapter.

The two final options—`Transaction Report` and `Check Writing`—are also useful; they dictate what will happen when you have finished entering and editing transactions. The former causes a transaction report to be generated when you save transactions, and the latter directs the system directly into check-writing mode.

Common Problems in Entering Transactions

Dollars and Sense simplifies transaction entry in several ways, but you may run into difficulties eventually. As you search for the answer to your problem, remember that the data you have entered is safe. Only real effort can destroy transactions once they have been entered. You are unlikely to lose anything even by switching off the computer in the middle of a session. Do *not*, however, switch off when the `saving data` message is displayed or when the disk drive's red light is on.

For those who have never entered transactions into Dollars and Sense, here are a few possible problems and advice on how to handle them.

1. *You try to distribute a transaction to a nonexistent account.* New users who have yet to establish the ideal set of accounts often have this problem. The only answer is to create an Account to correct the problem. You can remove the errant transaction, save other new transactions, go to the Account definitions window to create a new Account, then return to the entry screen to try again.

   You can leave the new transaction "undistributed" (see below) and create a new Account when the current entry session is over. At that time, use the edit transactions screen to recover the undistributed transaction and distribute the transaction properly. Moving from screen to screen takes less time than you might think.

   As part of your first Account list, you can create an ASSET Account called "Undistributed." Distribute to this Account all transactions that do not yet have an Account. Later, after you have created the necessary Accounts, open the "Undistributed" Account and reassign the transactions.

2. *You need more CHECK Accounts.* New users often think they can have only one CHECK Account, but you may have as many as 12. Create new CHECK Accounts in the Account definitions screen. Give the new Accounts a name, a number (preferably in the 100s), and enter *CHECK* in the `type` field.

3. *You want to enter a transaction into an EXPENSE or INCOME Account, but the program will not find the Account for you.* Transactions can be entered directly into only three types of Accounts: CHECK, LIABILITY, and ASSET, also known as Base Accounts. To appear in an EXPENSE or INCOME Account, a record must get there indirectly—by way of a Base Account.

4. *You have entered nearly 100 transactions, and the computer refuses to take more.* No more than 100

transactions—or to be more accurate, lines—can be stored per session. At that point, you reach the limits of temporary memory but not the limits of transaction storage. Save the transactions made, then redisplay the screen and enter any remaining transactions.

Entering Transactions in a CHECK Account

The most frequently used Base Account is a CHECK Account because transactions most often involve writing checks or depositing money in a bank checking account.

The window used to enter these transactions looks like a checkbook register (fig. 3.4). There are fields for all important aspects of a transaction: check number, date, description of payee, and at the far right, columns that show check or deposit amounts. You can record details of deposits, checks, and miscellaneous transactions in these columns.

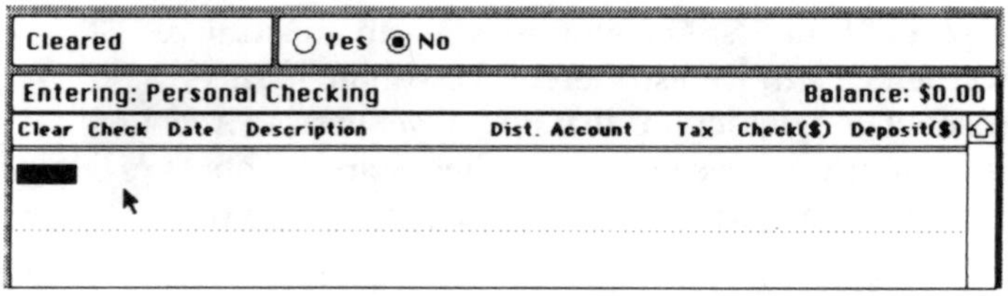

Fig. 3.4. The entry window for CHECK Accounts.

Transactions, once entered into this window, can be edited, added to your Dollars and Sense data base, or removed. Macintosh users do not enter transaction details directly into the fields, but point to the field in a box at the top of the screen. Entries are confirmed by pressing tab. Deposits and miscellaneous transactions are indicated by pointing and clicking the mouse on the `Deposit` or `Miscellaneous` buttons in the box. Distributions are created by clicking the mouse on the `Multiple` button.

Remember that you can enter a maximum of 100 transactions per session in any Dollars and Sense Base Account. At that point, you must save your work and start a new session. (On the Macintosh, you would select `New Transactions`. On the Apple, you are returned to the Main Menu.)

The Account name and its current balance are displayed at the top of the screen. When you update your check register, you probably calculate a current balance for each new transaction; in the entry screen, Dollars and Sense calculates the balance for you. As the current balance changes with each transaction, you can see how your checks and deposits affect the Account.

Notice the column headings of the entry window, from left to right.

1. `Clear`. This column, reserved for indicating transactions cleared by the bank, is empty when you first enter transactions. The letter `C` in this column indicates a cleared transaction.

2. `Check`. When you enter a transaction into a CHECK Account, you must decide whether the transaction is a check, a deposit, or neither. With a check, either write the check's number in the column, or accept the default. With a deposit, enter *D*. Enter a transaction that is neither, such as an electronic transaction made by your bank, as Miscellaneous.

   Checks can be numbered automatically, but you must set the first number or its equivalent in the CHECK Account data window. You can either accept a number or replace the number. When you replace the number, Dollars and Sense picks up the new sequence.

3. `Date`. Dates can also be supplied automatically. Depending on your system, the date supplied is either that of the last entry or a date written in an Account selection window. When, as is often necessary, you override the default with a new date, Dollars and Sense picks up the new sequence.

4. `Description`. You record a description of the check, deposit, or miscellaneous transaction in the description field. For a check, the description is usually of the payee. The source of a deposit, such as "Internal Revenue" (a tax refund) is usually mentioned. A miscellaneous transaction could be called "Electronic Transfer."

5. `Dist. Account`. Use the Distribution Account field to specify to which Account an amount is distributed. The distribution concept, central to Dollars and Sense, is discussed later in this chapter.

6. `Tax`. The Tax field is most commonly used to flag both tax-deductible and taxable amounts. Reports of all Tax transactions give you a detailed picture of your income and expenditures as you fill out your tax returns. The `Tax` is a label that need not be used for taxes. Some people use `Tax` to flag all business transactions.

7. `Check($)`, `Deposit($)`. The Check($) and Deposit($) columns display, respectively, subtractions from and additions to a Base Account. With the "multidistributed" items discussed later in this chapter, these columns show two sides of a distribution rather than subtractions from and additions to a Base Account.

Hands-On Hints

Entering Transactions

Transactions can be entered when the entry screen is in `new` mode.

The Apple Family

Check numbers and the date may be supplied automatically. Accept them with Return, Enter or tab, or override them. Press *M* or *D* in the `CHK#` field for a miscellaneous transaction or a deposit. When a field is filled, the cursor moves to the next field. If your entry does not fill a field, press Return, Enter, or tab to confirm that the entry is complete. Write a description of the transaction. Select a distribution Account, or use the asterisk key to split the transaction between more than one Account. Flag tax-related transactions or distributed amounts with *T*. Enter the amount of the check, the deposit, or the distributed segments. Switch to `edit` mode, then save the transactions.

Searching and Scrolling

Searching and scrolling, a timesaving operating technique that recurs in several contexts in Dollars and Sense, functions in the Distribution Account field of the entry window.

After you have established your Accounts, you will rarely need to write a complete name to find an Account. In many situations, you need type only the first few letters of an Account name, then confirm the entry with Return. Dollars and Sense searches the Account list and supplies the complete name. When the first few letters of two names are identical, Dollars and Sense supplies the first alphabetical listing. Should this not be the Account you need, press the horizontal arrow keys to make each Account name appear in alphabetical order. (Macintosh users must press the Apple key with the greater than (>) or less than (<) keys for the same effect.)

This is known as "scrolling," a term peculiar to the computer world. The closest analogy is an alphabetical list written on a conveyor belt. Your Accounts, now that you have established them, have become like that list, and the arrow keys scroll either forward or backward through the list. The right-arrow key runs forward through the sequence, the left-arrow key goes in the opposite direction.

Simple Check Distribution

Multiple record keeping is the only reasonable way to keep close control of financial records. Dollars and Sense is a multiple record keeping system, and the program has the capability to distribute a transaction to different accounts.

"Distributing a transaction" can mean different things in different situations. On the simplest level, distributing a transaction means that a record of the transaction is kept in more than one Account, with a resultant change in Account balances. Sometimes a distribution Account signifies where money is going, at other times where the money comes from. Sometimes the money is not being transferred, and the distribution Account simply keeps a record of the amount.

To summarize the effects of distributing a check to other Accounts when the Base Account is a CHECK Account:

> *Checks.* A check *decreases* the balance of the Base Account and of any LIABILITY or INCOME Account to which the check is distributed. When a check is distributed to any EXPENSE, ASSET, or CHECK Account, the transaction *increases* their balances.

Specific examples should clarify this general rule.

Distributing a Transaction to a LIABILITY Account

Suppose you write a $30 check to pay off part of your debt to VISA (fig. 3.5). Specify "Personal Checking" or its equivalent as the Base Account and make sure that the check default is set correctly. Then display the entry screen. Reading from your check register, enter details of the transaction to the screen.

Entering: Personal Checking

Clear	Check	Date	Description	Dist. Account	Tax	Check($)	Deposit($)
	8002	01/12	VISA payment	VISA	-	30.00	

Fig. 3.5. Distributing a transaction to a LIABILITY Account.

By writing the check, you have reduced by $30 the balances of your Personal Checking Account and of your VISA Account (a LIABILITY Account). If (using a transaction summary) you display the transactions in the VISA Account, you will see that Dollars and Sense has both done and recorded the work for you.

Distributing a Transaction to an EXPENSE Account

Distributing a check to an EXPENSE Account has a different effect. Suppose you write a check for $50 at the market. Again, the Base Account is Personal Checking (fig. 3.6). By writing the check, you have reduced the balance of your Personal Checking Account and increased the balance of the Groceries Account accordingly. The Groceries Account is an EXPENSE Account; this Account simply keeps a running tally of what has been spent.

Entering: Personal Checking

Clear	Check	Date	Description	Dist. Account	Tax	Check($)	Deposit($)
-	8001	01/12	Vegimart	Groceries	-	50.00	

Fig. 3.6. Distributing a transaction to an EXPENSE Account.

The change in the Groceries Account is easily demonstrated if you now use a transaction summary to display the transactions in the Account (fig. 3.7). The Account has been updated with the $50 just entered, Personal Checking is the source of the money in the Distribution Account column, and the Account balance is appropriately increased.

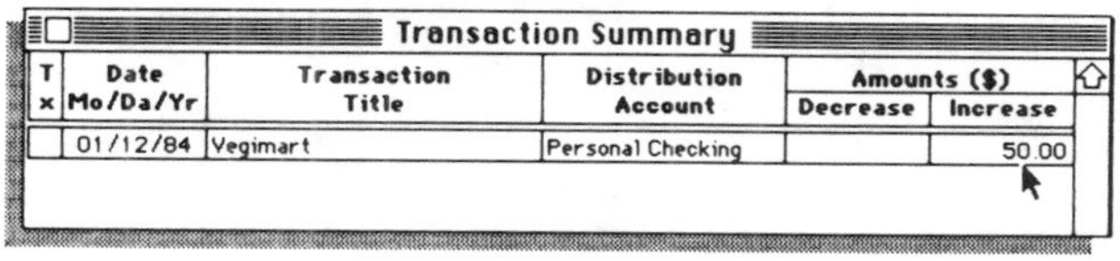

Transaction Summary
T x
Date Mo/Da/Yr
Transaction Title
Distribution Account
Amounts ($)
Decrease
Increase
01/12/84
Vegimart
Personal Checking
50.00

Fig. 3.7. A transaction summary of the Groceries Account.

Distributing a Transaction to Another CHECK Account

When you write a check to transfer money from one Account to another, there are two ways to record the event. Depending on what you have in mind, you can write the transfer as a check transaction in the "from" Account, or as a deposit in the "to" Account. (The advantage of the deposit method is discussed at length in Chapter 5.)

To transfer funds from your Checking Account to a Money Market Account, record the transaction by following the example in figure 3.8.

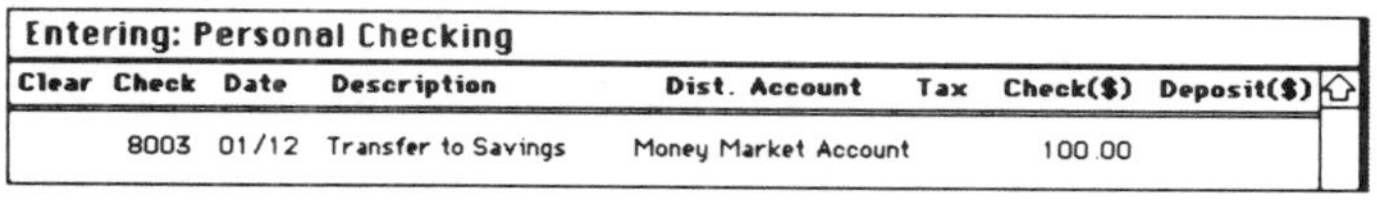

Fig. 3.8. Distributing a transaction to another CHECK Account.

This transaction reduces the balance of the Personal Checking Account and increases the balance of the Money Market Account. You can verify this by examining the Money Market Account (using `Past Transactions`). The transfer has been recorded with `Special` in the Check column to indicate that the money was originally entered in a different Base Account (fig. 3.9).

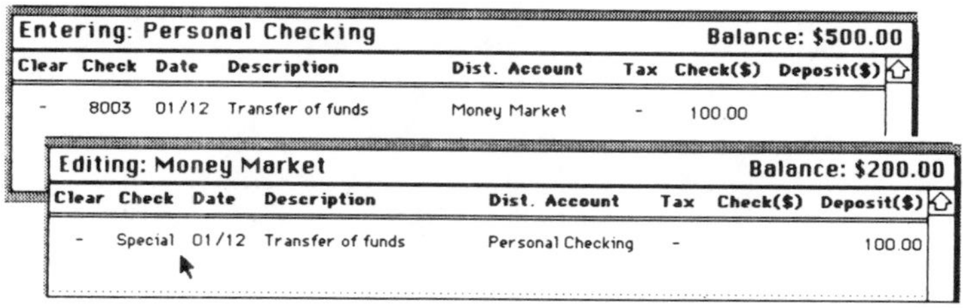

Entering: Personal Checking
Balance: $500.00
Clear
Check
Date
Description
Dist. Account
Tax
Check($)
Deposit($)
-
8003
01/12
Transfer of funds
Money Market
-
100.00
Editing: Money Market
Balance: $200.00
Clear
Check
Date
Description
Dist. Account
Tax
Check($)
Deposit($)
-
Special
01/12
Transfer of funds
Personal Checking
-
100.00

Fig. 3.9. A `Special` *transaction from CHECK Account to CHECK Account.*

Hands-On Hints

Editing Transactions

Transactions can be edited when the entry screen is in edit mode.

Apple II, II+, and IIe

Switch from the new mode to edit mode by pressing the F key. To move around the screen, use arrow keys or press the Control key and certain letter keys simultaneously.

1. Control-K tabs up a line.
2. Control-J tabs down a line.
3. Control-B displays the first page.
4. Control-P displays the next page.

When the cursor is at the field to be changed, replace the original entry with a new one and confirm, if necessary, with Return. Press the R key to remove or restore a transaction or distribution. When finished, save the edits by pressing the Q key and then the Y key.

Apple IIc

Press Escape to switch from the new to edit mode. Move around the screen with the arrow keys. Press Apple-B, or use the mouse, to return to a previous field. When the cursor is at the field to be changed, replace the original entry with a new one and confirm, if necessary, with Return. Press the R key to remove or restore a transaction or distribution. When finished, save the edits by pressing Escape, then continuing.

Simple Deposit Distribution

The effect of distributing a deposit also varies according to the type of Account involved. The rules are a mirror image of those that apply to checks.

> Deposits. A deposit to a checking Account *increases* the balance of the Base Account and any INCOME or LIABILITY Account to which the deposit is distributed. The deposit will *decrease* the balance of any ASSET or EXPENSE Account to which the deposit is distributed.

To understand simple deposit distributions, see figures 3.10 and 3.11 and the accompanying explanations.

Distributing a Deposit to an INCOME Account

When you receive a Christmas bonus and deposit the money in Personal Checking (fig. 3.10), the balances of two Accounts, Personal Checking and Gross Income, are increased.

Fig. 3.10. Distribution to an INCOME Account.

Entering: Personal Checking

Clear	Check	Date	Description	Dist. Account	Tax	Check($)	Deposit($)
	Deposit	01/14	Bonus From Office	Gross Income		900.00	

This does not mean that you have doubled your money! INCOME Accounts merely keep track, for tax reporting and planning purposes, of how much has been earned. Incidentally, when you enter this transaction you could also flag it in the appropriate column with *T*, which marks the transaction as a tax-related item.

Distributing a Deposit to a CHECK Account

Another way to record transfers is to show them as deposits in the receiving account (fig. 3.11). Because this transaction is a deposit, the distribution account indicates where the funds come from. This time the balance of the Personal Checking Account has been increased and the Savings Account has been decreased.

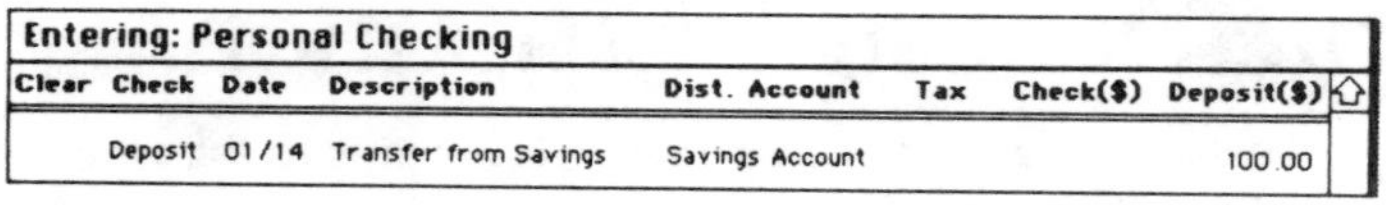
Entering: Personal Checking
Clear Check Date Description Dist. Account Tax Check($) Deposit($)
Deposit 01/14 Transfer from Savings Savings Account 100.00

Fig. 3.11. Distribution to a CHECK Account.

Multiple Account Check Distributions

You have seen how simple distributions affect different types of Accounts. The rules also apply to multiple Account distributions. Sometimes a single transaction has several components, each of which must be distributed to a different Account. Theoretically, you could distribute a transaction to as many as 14 different Accounts.

When you buy a load of bricks and a bottle of Drano at the hardware store, you are likely to use one check. The purchases can be recorded in two different Accounts—Home Improvement and Household Expenses. Dollars and Sense lets you record this as a single transaction in the Base Account while, at the same time, recording two separate transactions in the other Accounts. The Macintosh Multiple button commands the program to begin the distribution (fig. 3.12).

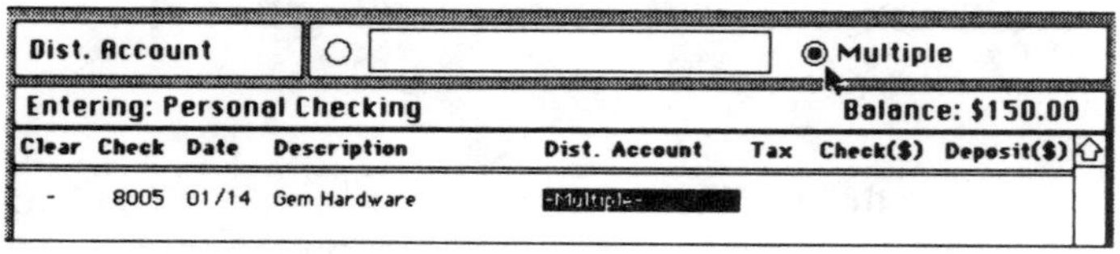
Dist. Account
Multiple
Entering: Personal Checking
Balance: $150.00
Clear Check Date Description Dist. Account Tax Check($) Deposit($)
- 8005 01/14 Gem Hardware -Multiple-

Fig. 3.12. The Multiple button begins a distribution.

This one transaction is now recorded in three Accounts (fig. 3.13). The Personal Checking balance has been decreased by $62; Household is increased by $2; Home Improvement is increased by $60. Macintosh helps you by calculating what is needed to balance the distribution. Macintosh saves you the trouble of making these calculations yourself.

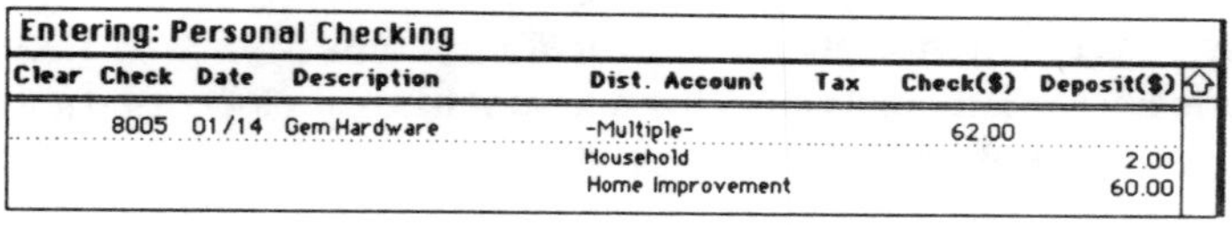
Entering: Personal Checking
Clear Check Date Description Dist. Account Tax Check($) Deposit($)
8005 01/14 Gem Hardware -Multiple- 62.00
Household 2.00
Home Improvement 60.00

Fig. 3.13. A multiple Account distribution.

Balancing Distributions

At first glance the way in which distributions are displayed can be confusing. The two smaller amounts appear in the `Deposit` column, but these amounts are not actually deposited in the Base Account (Personal Checking). The figures simply show the breakdown of the total amount of the check.

There are three important points to remember when you balance distributions:

1. Both sides of the equation must balance. The amounts on the right side must equal those on the left. Dollars and Sense tells you if the distribution does not balance. You can rebalance a distribution either by changing amounts or by switching them from one column to another, depending on the problem. (The *S* key or the switch button make the switch.)
2. The first term in a multiple Account distribution dictates whether the distribution reduces or increases the balance of the Base Account.
3. The columns in which the distribution amounts appear determine whether these amounts increase or decrease the balances of distribution Accounts. Generally speaking, the left column denotes a decrease, the right denotes an increase. (In figure 3.13, for example, the amount that reduces the Base Account appears in the left column. That amount is balanced by the two amounts that increase the distribution accounts in the right column.) If you are distributing a check to the LIABILITY Account, however, the result would be a reduced balance, because adding money to a liability has the same effect as paying off a debt.

Hands-On Hints

Multiple Account Distribution of Checks

The Apple Family

After entering and confirming the transaction description, press the shift and asterisk keys at the same time to signal a multiple distribution. Then enter the amount of the check. When you confirm the amount, the cursor goes to the next Distribution Account field. Enter a name for the first distribution Account by searching and scrolling. When you enter the distribution amounts, they appear (for display reasons only) in the `Deposit` column. After you have found all the distribution accounts, you can finish by again pressing shift and the asterisk key. An even quicker method is to press Return on the last amount field. Dollars and Sense computes the last amount for you and closes the distribution.

Multiple Account Deposit Distributions

Deposits can also be broken up and distributed between different accounts. The perfect example of this is a paycheck composed of a number of elements that must be recorded separately for you to keep your Base Account properly balanced and for tax purposes.

The net amount of a paycheck actually increases the balance of the Base Account and must be distinguished from the gross amount. EXPENSE Accounts record withholding. In California, the distribution will appear as in figure 3.14 (different states may have different requirements).

Editing: Personal Checking

Clear	Check	Date	Description	Dist. Account	Tax	Check($)	Deposit($)
-	Deposit	01/14	Monogram	-Multiple-	-		2,456.00
				Gross Income	T	3,300.00	
				Taxes - Federal	T		500.00
				Taxes - State	T		90.00
				FICA	T		235.00
				Medical Plan	T		19.00

Fig. 3.14. Distribution of a paycheck.

The description indicates the source of the check, in this case the company that employs you. The first amount is the actual net amount of the check, which is deposited directly into the Personal Checking Account.

The distribution shown in figure 3.14 also increases by the gross amount the balance of the Gross Income Account, thus keeping a running total of before-tax income earned. Gross Income also acts as a balancing Account that enables other distributions to be made. The remaining four sums go to increase the balances of EXPENSE Accounts. At the end of the year these balances will be useful for preparing your tax return. Once more, note how the two sides of the equation balance.

In this distribution, every term but the first (net income) is flagged with T to show that these amounts are tax-related.

Undistributed and Undistributable Transactions

An occasional transaction is relevant to one Account only and need not be distributed (fig. 3.15).

Fig. 3.15. An undistributed transaction.

Entering: Personal Checking

Clear	Check	Date	Description	Dist. Account	Tax	Check($)	Deposit($)
-	Deposit	01/14	Gift from George	Undistributed	-		100.00

This transaction records a birthday gift, deposited directly into a CHECK Account. The balance of the Base Account is increased by $100. The check is too small to declare for taxes, and there is no reason to record the check elsewhere.

For all systems, transactions are undistributed if you enter nothing in the Distribution Account field and confirm the entry with tab, Return, or Enter, according to the system.

Electronic Transactions

With the growth of home banking services, miscellaneous transactions are increasingly common. To call them checks or deposits is accurate only in the sense that they reduce or increase an account balance. Calling them "miscellaneous" is more convenient, because paperwork is rarely involved in the initial transaction. For example, automatic teller withdrawals reduce the balance of an Account but have no check number (fig. 3.16).

Fig. 3.16. A withdrawal from an automatic teller machine.

Entering: Personal Checking

Clear	Check	Date	Description	Dist. Account	Tax	Check($)	Deposit($)
-	Misc	01/14	Autoteller quick cash	Cash	-	40.00	

This transaction reduces the Base Account by $40, increasing the Cash on Hand Account accordingly. In this case, write the amount in the Check column.

A miscellaneous deposit, such as an electronic transfer of funds, must be recorded with the amount in the Deposit column (fig. 3.17). The amount does not appear in that column unless you "shift" it there. With Macintosh check the Switch Column box at the top of the screen. (The S key has the same effect on other machines.) Dollars and Sense "knows" it is dealing with a deposit only when the amount has switched columns.

Deposit Amount 200.00 ☒ Switch Column

Entering: Personal Checking Balance: $2,504.00

Clear	Check	Date	Description	Dist. Account	Tax	Check($)	Deposit($)
-	Misc	01/14	Transfer	Money Market	-		200.00

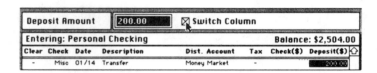

Fig. 3.17. A miscellaneous deposit.

Cash Management

Plastic may be the currency of the future, but cash is still the most convenient way to pay your small everyday expenses. You can keep track of your cash on hand by using one of the ready-made Household Accounts, the ASSET Account called Cash.

Withdrawing Cash

When you cash a check, record the transaction as shown in figure 3.18.

Entering: Personal Checking

Clear	Check	Date	Description	Dist. Account	Tax	Check($)	Deposit($)
-	8032	02/08	Ace Liquors	Cash	-	25.00	

Fig. 3.18. Cashing a check.

This transaction decreases the balance of your CHECK Account while increasing the cash in your pocket, represented by the Cash ASSET Account.

Figure 3.19 shows what happens when you deposit a check at the bank and withdraw part of the check as cash.

Entering: Personal Checking

Clear	Check	Date	Description	Dist. Account	Tax	Check($)	Deposit($)
-	Deposit	02/09	Sunset Magazine	-Multiple-	-		450.00
				Gross Income	T	500.00	
				Cash	T		50.00

Fig. 3.19. Partial cash withdrawal from a deposit.

To track how much you have earned, the face value of the check (the gross amount) must be recorded in Gross Income. The transaction credits Personal Checking with $450 and increases the Cash ASSET Account by $50.

Spending Cash

You must use Cash as the Base Account to record cash purchases. Because this is an ASSET Account, the entry screen looks different (fig. 3.20).

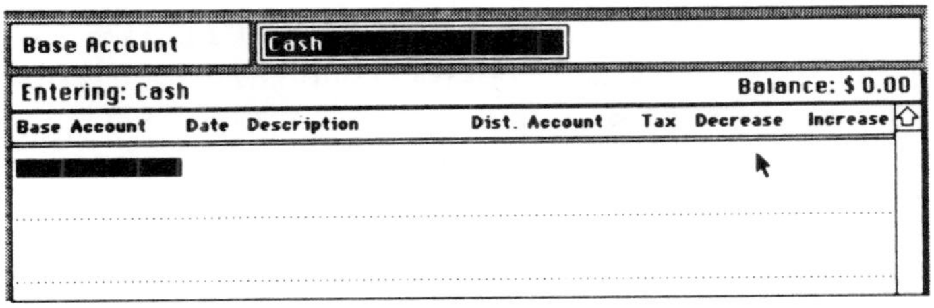

Fig. 3.20. The transaction entry window for an ASSET Account.

Account entry screens, ASSET and LIABILITY included, record increases to and decreases from the Base Account balance. Notice that, as with the LIABILITY entry screen, the Account name appears at extreme left. The major difference here is that the amount columns are actually labeled Decrease and Increase, as opposed to Checks and Deposits or Purchases and Payments. The Balance figure in this case should correspond exactly to the amount of cash you have on hand.

Figure 3.21 shows how Dollars and Sense records cash payment for an article of clothing. The expense is recorded in Clothing, cash on hand has been depleted by $50, and the amount has been shifted to appear in the proper column.

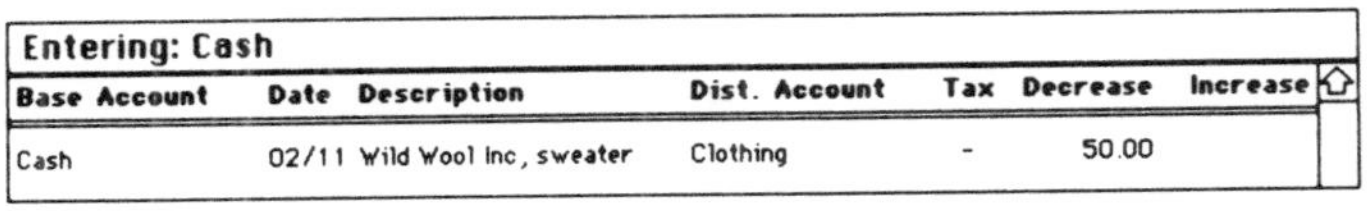

Fig. 3.21. Recording a cash purchase.

You can even make a multiple Account distribution in an ASSET Base Account when you pay cash for two items that must be recorded separately (fig. 3.22). Logically, you could enter them as two separate transactions, but the distribution method is marginally quicker. (Remember to shift the first amount to the Decrease column.)

Entering: Cash

Base Account	Date	Description	Dist. Account	Tax	Decrease	Increase
Cash	02/12	Big Store Inc.	-Multiple-	-	75.00	
			Bus. Equip.	-		30.00
			Furniture	-		45.00

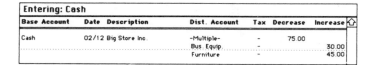

Fig. 3.24. The TRANSACTION REPORT QUERY box.

Saving Transactions

After you have entered transactions, you can save them as part of the Dollars and Sense data base. When you choose End Edit from the Edit Menu, Macintosh displays a dialog box for confirming your selection. You can also use this box to start three follow-up operations: a report of the new transactions, check writing, or saving the transactions as an automatic set (fig. 3.23).

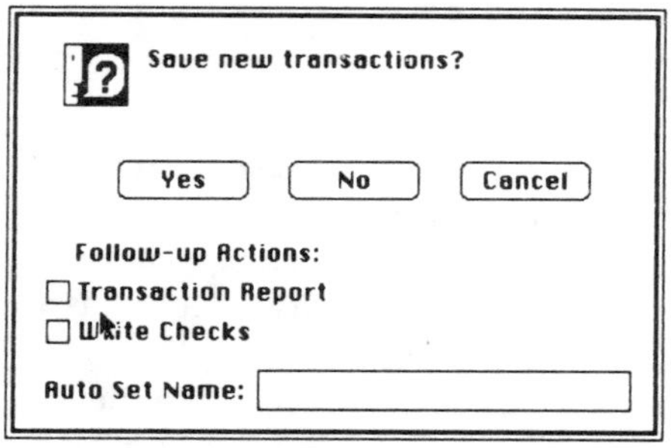

Fig. 3.25. The TRANSACTION REPORT box.

While Dollars and Sense takes a few moments to store the transactions, a warning appears on screen. This is one of the few times that you must not switch off your computer.

Hands-On Hints

Saving Transactions

Apple II, II+, and IIe

With the screen in edit mode, press the Q key to quit. The screen changes to give you three choices: Continue, Exit, or Save. Press the S key to save transactions.

Apple IIc

With the screen in edit mode, press the S key or click the mouse on `Save`. When the `Are you ready to save all updates. . .` ? message appears, select `Yes`.

Instant Feedback with Transaction Reports

The transaction report is probably the first Dollars and Sense report you will encounter or need. Using an Account selection screen or its variant, you can set up the system to produce a report of any new transactions as soon as you have saved them. At any time, by selecting from the Report Menu, you can create a full report of any group of stored transactions.

Take full advantage of the transaction report, a diverse and powerful money management tool. A transaction report gives you a quick, convenient, and comprehensive picture of your financial activity and your current balances. With the Transaction Report Query box, these reports can also detail every transaction you make, break them down into many smaller categories, or even hunt down a single transaction (fig. 3.24).

You can, for example, create transaction reports to show:

1. Transactions in any Account, for any date or number range
2. All tax-related transactions in an Account
3. All transactions in an Account for a particular week or month
4. Checks written to any payee, such as a grocery or clothing store
5. A check, or checks, written for a specific amount
6. All deposits for any date range
7. All automatic teller transactions

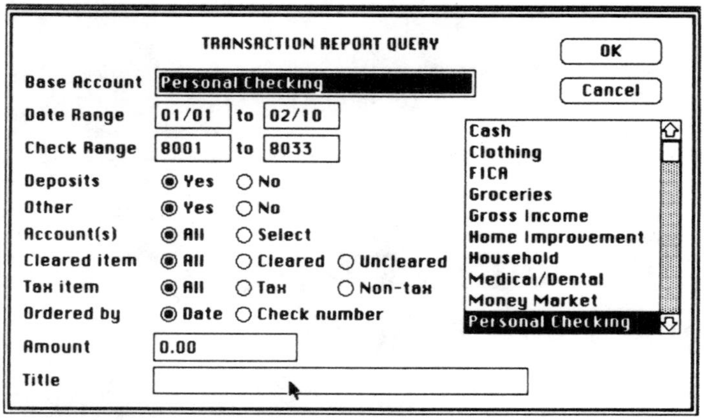

Fig. 3.24. The Transaction Report Query box.

Because of its capability to recall transaction descriptions and extract detailed reports from any Account, Dollars and Sense reduces the number of Accounts you must create. For example, you can use a single entertainment Account for both personal and business expenses. A transaction report can find all business-related expenses if you "key" the transactions as you enter them. For example, when you record a transaction for a business-related expense, simply include the word *business* (or *bus.*) in the description field.

After you have selected the report's parameters and clicked the OK box, the Transaction Report box appears (fig. 3.25). You now decide how the report will appear: with all transaction lines, including distributions; without distributions; or as a summary of what the specified transactions contribute to each Account.

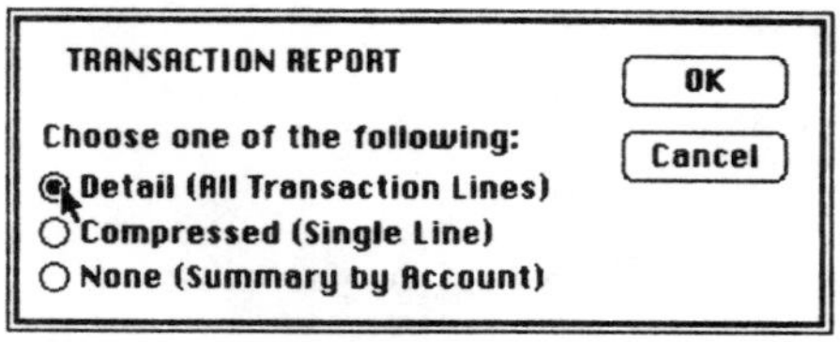

Fig. 3.25. The Transaction Report box.

Transaction reports have two parts: the Transaction Summary and the Account YTD (Year-To-Date) Summary. The Transaction Summary is a record of transactions in either date order or order of deposits (fig. 3.26). A full report also shows distributions, whereas a compressed report shows only the total amounts of each transaction.

Transaction Summary

C 1	T x	Check Num	Date Mo/Da	Transaction Title	Distribution Account	Amounts ($) Check	Deposit
		8001	01/12	Vegimart	Groceries	50.00	
		8003	01/12	Transfer of funds	Money Market	100.00	
		Deposit	01/14	Monogram			2,456.00
					Gross Income	3,300.00	
	T				Taxes - Federal		500.00
	T				Taxes - State		90.00
	T				FICA		235.00
					Medical/Dental		19.00
		Deposit	01/14	Gift from George	Undistributed		100.00
			01/14	Autoteller quick cash	Cash	40.00	
			01/14	Transfer	Money Market	200.00	
		8005	01/14	Gem Hardware		62.00	
					Household		2.00
					Home Improvement		60.00
		8032	02/08	Ace Liquors	Cash	25.00	
		Deposit	02/09	Sunset Magazine			450.00
	T				Gross Income	500.00	
	T				Cash		50.00
			02/10	Autoteller cash	Cash	50.00	
		8033	02/10	test	Groceries	50.00	

Fig. 3.26. A typical Transaction Summary.

The Account YTD Summary, a summary of how the transactions affect individual Accounts, shows the number of transactions, their total amount, and the current balance of the Account (fig. 3.27). The tax balance is also shown. This is particularly useful if you choose only tax-related items in the query.

Account YTD Summary

Accounts Num	Name	Type	Number Tran..	Total Amount	Current Balance
100	Personal Checking	Check	11	2,429.00	2,429.00
110	Money Market	Check	2	300.00	400.00
200	Cash	Asset	4	165.00	40.00
420	Gross Income	Income	2	3,800.00	3,800.00
540	FICA	Expense	1	235.00	235.00
550	Groceries	Expense	2	100.00	100.00
560	Household	Expense	1	2.00	47.00
580	Medical/Dental	Expense	1	19.00	19.00
610	Taxes - Federal	Expense	1	500.00	500.00
630	Taxes - State	Expense	1	90.00	90.00
641	Home Improvement	Expense	1	60.00	60.00

Fig. 3.27. The Account YTD Summary.

A transaction report can detail as many as 1,000 transactions. If you need to see more than 1,000 transactions, separate them into groups with the "transaction query criteria" discussed later in this chapter. When you ask for transactions listed by check number, the first 1,000 check numbers appear.

In figure 3.27 the *Total Amount* column represents the sum of transactions covered by the report in each Account. In this example, the total amount for personal checking equals the current balance because the report covers the complete range of transactions in that Account.

Hands-On Hints

Creating Transaction Reports

Apple II, II+, and IIe

In the Main Menu, select Option E. When the Transaction Report Menu appears, select Option A and specify which Account you want to report on. Set any parameters, such as a date- or check-range, and proceed. When the `Select Output Device` screen appears, specify `screen` or `printer` and whether the report is to show distributions `Full` or `Compressed`. Proceed to the report. Press the P key to see successive pages of the report.

Apple IIc

In the Main Menu, select Option E. When the Transaction Report Menu appears, select Option A and specify which Account you want to report on. Set any parameters, such as a date- or check-range, and proceed. When the Transaction Detail Menu appears, specify `screen` or `printer` and whether the report will show distributions `Full` or `Compressed`. You can also ask for an Account Summary. Press Return to see successive pages of the report.

The Power of Transaction Report Criteria

Transaction criteria, displayed either as a menu or in a Macintosh box, are the means by which you can specify which transactions you want to recall. Each criterion has a specific function, but you can combine the criteria to focus accurately on your target. Used properly, report criteria can isolate a single transaction in the data base.

1. `Date Range`. To recall transactions from a particular time period, set a beginning and end for the date range. Otherwise, all transactions in the account are recalled.

2. `Check Range`. You can recall any range of check numbers by entering both beginning and end numbers. For a

report of only deposits and miscellaneous transactions, exclude checks by making the beginning number larger than the ending number. If you set no check range, all checks will appear.

3. `Deposits`. You can include or exclude deposits from the report. In menu configurations, selecting the `Deposits` option acts as a "toggle," repeatedly switching the deposit status off and on.

4. `Other`. This option refers to miscellaneous transactions. For a report of all such miscellaneous transactions, such as electronic bill payments and automatic teller withdrawals and transfers, switch on the `Other` option and switch off `Deposits` and `Check Range`.

5. `Ordered by`. Transactions can be made to appear in order of date or check number. In check number order, deposits and miscellaneous transactions appear first.

6. `Tax item`. A report of tax-related items is often useful, especially as the time to report taxes draws near. Your use of this option depends on whether the report is to include only tax-related transactions, all items, or items that have nothing to do with taxes.

7. `Cleared Item`. Cleared items are transactions cleared during bank statement reconciliation. You can produce a report of cleared, uncleared, or all transactions. A report of uncleared items indicates which transactions have yet to appear on your bank statement.

8. `Title`. This powerful search capability helps you find a particular transaction or group of transactions. Dollars and Sense searches for entries in the description field that could match the title you enter here. Suppose, for example, that you wrote a check to the Gem Hardware store, recorded the transaction in Dollars and Sense, but have no other record of the check. Enter *Gem* in the title field, and Dollars and Sense will find the transaction for you. Instead of the name of the store, you can enter *hardware*, or just *har* (fig. 3.28). Dollars and Sense would still find the transaction because the program identifies descriptions by means of a "string" search that looks for a sequence of three characters. These characters can be separated by a space, but not by a period.

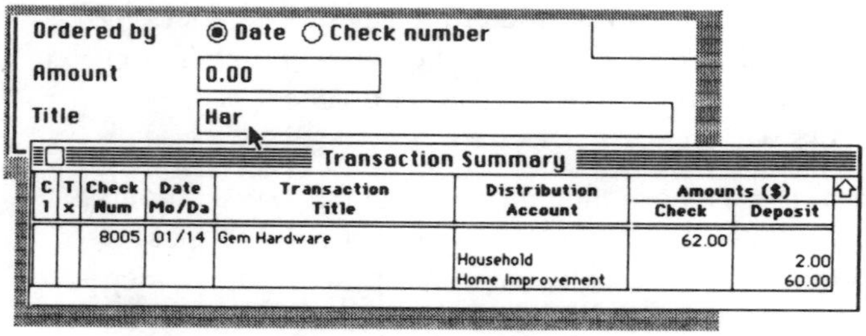

Fig. 3.28. A transaction found by a partial `Title` *search.*

9. `Amount`. Dollars and Sense can also search the data base for a particular amount. Suppose that you cannot remember exactly when you deposited $55 through the automatic teller. Enter *$55* in the amount field for a report of all $55 transactions within the date range. It should be easy to pick out the record you need.

10. `Accounts`. When this criterion is set at `All`, reports will detail Base Account transactions that relate to all Accounts. You can, however, find transactions that relate only to a particular Account. For example, you may want details of your mortgage interest payments for a given period. Enter *Mortgage Interest* in the accounts field (searching and scrolling works here too) to see a report of mortgage interest transactions. A full report will also show mortgage principal payments associated with the transactions. The summary also shows all related Accounts (in this case, the Base Account, and both the Mortgage and Mortgage Interest Accounts).

4
The Monthly Session

At least once a month your Dollars and Sense session will include familiar but not always welcome tasks such as bill payment and bank account reconciliation. The monthly session is also a good time to see whether your budgets are working and to increase or decrease the budgets accordingly.

Paying Bills

Probably the only bills you ever enjoy paying are the final installments of mortgages and loans. Paying other bills is traumatic, and most of us grit our teeth and endure the monthly ritual. Dollars and Sense does not make paying bills enjoyable but does make the process easier, particularly with "automatic" transactions and "automatic" check writing capabilities.

Before discussing these capabilities, we will look at some typical bills—mortgage, car loan, gas, electricity, water, telephone, and child care. You can use Personal Checking, the medium of payment, as the Base Account to record payment of these bills in Dollars and Sense.

Mortgage Payments

For many Americans a mortgage is their largest monthly expenditure. The major portion of a mortgage payment covers interest. Because the Internal Revenue Service allows mortgage interest as a tax deduction, be sure to record separately your interest and principal payments. The other Account in the distribution, Mortgage Insurance, is offered by the mortgage company (fig. 4.1). (The face amount of this term policy decreases to coincide with the rate of mortgage repayment.)

Entering: Personal Checking

Clear	Check	Date	Description	Dist. Account	Tax	Check($)	Deposit($)
-	8010	01/30	Western Finance	-Multiple-	-	820.00	
				Mortgage	-		20.00
				Mortgage Interest	T		750.00
				Mortgage Insur.	-		50.00

Fig. 4.1. Distribution of a mortgage payment

The amount of your monthly check appears in the Check column; the Deposit column shows the payment's three components. The $820 reduces the balance of the Personal Checking Account. The $20 reduces the balance of the Mortgage LIABILITY Account. The $750 increases the balance of the Mortgage Interest EXPENSE Account, which keeps track of the interest you pay. Be sure to flag the $750 with T. The $50 increases the balance of the Mortgage Insurance EXPENSE Account, a record of what you have spent on insurance.

Car Payments

As with your mortgage, you must record other loans as separate principal and interest payments. Make your Car Loan a LIABILITY Account and use as your starting balance the amount you owe when you open the Account. See figure 4.2 for an example of how to write a car loan payment.

Entering: Personal Checking

Clear	Check	Date	Description	Dist. Account	Tax	Check($)	Deposit($)
-	Misc	01/30	Ace Finance	-Multiple-	-	150.00	
				Car Loan	-		125.00
				Loan Interest	T		25.00

Fig. 4.2. Distribution of a car payment.

Record the transaction as Miscellaneous if the bank automatically subtracts the payment from your checking account. Because the figure appears in the Check($) column, Dollars and Sense "knows" the payment is a deduction from your checking account. If you pay by check, record the transaction accordingly.

Utility Payments

One Utilities Account should suffice for all utility payments because such payments are usually single distribution transactions (fig. 4.3). You can produce a transaction report of any individual description if you ever need to know how much you spend on individual utilities.

Fig. 4.3. Payments from the Utilities Account.

Entering: Personal Checking

Clear	Check	Date	Description	Dist. Account	Tax	Check($)	Deposit($)
-	8011	01/30	Gas Company	Utilities		50.00	
-	8012	01/30	Water Company	Utilities		25.00	
-	8013	01/30	Electric Company	Utilities		30.00	

Telephone Bill Payments

Payments to the telephone company can usually be recorded as simple transactions with one distribution Account (fig. 4.4).

Fig. 4.4. Paying your telephone bill.

Entering: Personal Checking

Clear	Check	Date	Description	Dist. Account	Tax	Check($)	Deposit($)
-	8012	01/30	Pacific Bell	Utilities	-	40.00	

For business calls made from home, you can create a Reimbursable Expenses Account and distribute the check differently (fig. 4.5). Use a transaction report as a bill to collect from your company the $10 recorded in Reimbursable Business Expenses. If you are self-employed, create a separate Business Phone Account.

Fig. 4.5. Distribution of a telephone payment with business calls.

Entering: Personal Checking

Clear	Check	Date	Description	Dist. Account	Tax	Check($)	Deposit($)
-	8012	01/30	Pacific Bell	-Multiple-	-	40.00	
				Utilities	-		30.00
				Reimb. Expenses	-		10.00

Child Care Payments

Keep a careful record of money spent on child care, because the payments can be claimed as a tax credit (fig. 4.6).

Fig. 4.6. Child care payment flagged with T.

Entering: Personal Checking

Clear	Check	Date	Description	Dist. Account	Tax	Check($)	Deposit($)
-	8014	01/30	Kidland	Child Care	T	120.00	

Paying Monthly Bills Automatically

The Dollars and Sense automatic transactions capability can help you with your monthly bills. Regular transactions need be written only once. The transactions can then be stored as a set and reactivated whenever appropriate. An automatic set (fig. 4.7) can contain as many as 100 transactions, and you can create up to 25 sets per file. When you recall the set, simply update it with new dates, check numbers, and—if necessary—amounts.

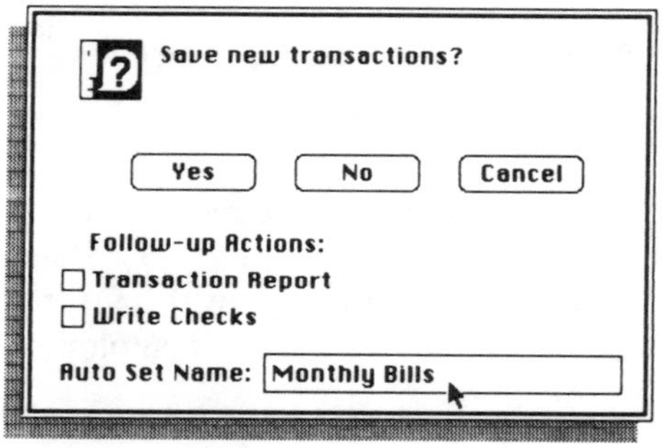

Fig. 4.7. Naming the automatic set.

With Macintosh, you create an automatic set by first naming the set in the entry window, then saving the set when the `Save new transactions?` box appears.

With other computers, create an automatic set by setting an option of the Account Selection Menu. The option switches on the automatic transactions feature, and the next transactions you write will be saved as an automatic set.

Hands-On Hints

Creating Automatic Transaction Sets

Apple II, II+, and IIe

In the Account Selection Menu, first specify the Base Account (the Account you use to write checks). If there are no automatic sets on the disk, choose Option D to display `Set 01 (New)`. Proceed to the entry screen, and the next set of transactions you enter will be an automatic set.

Apple IIc

In the Enter Transactions Menu, first specify the Base Account (the Account you use to write checks). If there are no automatic sets on the disk, choose Option E to display `Set 01 (New)`. Proceed to the entry screen, and the next set of transactions you enter will be an automatic set.

Reactivating the Set

Once the transactions are saved, they update Dollars and Sense records, are stored as an automatic set, and can be recalled to the screen when needed (fig. 4.8). After you recall automatic sets, use the Macintosh scroll box to select the set you need (fig. 4.9).

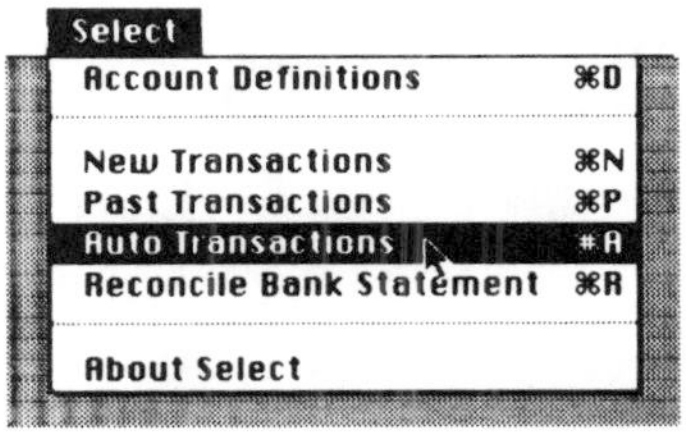

Fig. 4.8. Automatic sets are recalled by the Select Menu.

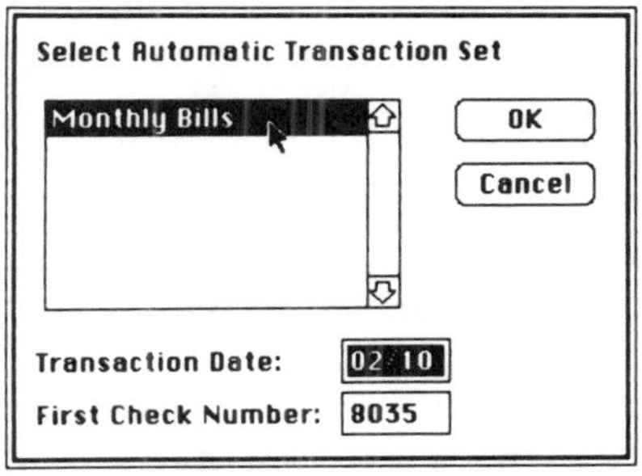

Fig. 4.9. The Macintosh scroll box for selecting automatic sets.

When automatic sets are recalled, Dollars and Sense indicates that the first amount is ready to be changed. You do not have to change the amount; but if you want to do so, the default saves you some work. Press tab, Return, or Enter to move the cursor to the next amount. The balance of your Base Account changes as you update amounts. These changes can alert you immediately to the chance of overextending your checking account.

After you have updated all the amounts, you can edit the set, changing dates, check numbers, and distributions when necessary (fig. 4.10). Saving the set updates the data base.

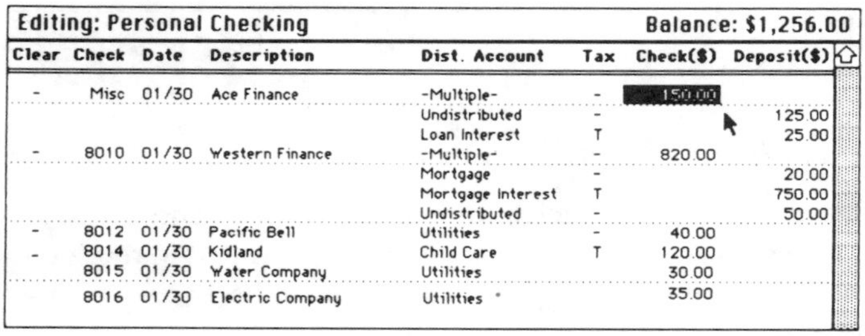
Editing: Personal Checking Balance: $1,256.00

Clear	Check	Date	Description	Dist. Account	Tax	Check($)	Deposit($)
-	Misc	01/30	Ace Finance	-Multiple-	-	150.00	
				Undistributed	-		125.00
				Loan Interest	T		25.00
-	8010	01/30	Western Finance	-Multiple-	-	820.00	
				Mortgage	-		20.00
				Mortgage Interest	T		750.00
				Undistributed	-		50.00
-	8012	01/30	Pacific Bell	Utilities	-	40.00	
-	8014	01/30	Kidland	Child Care	T	120.00	
	8015	01/30	Water Company	Utilities		30.00	
	8016	01/30	Electric Company	Utilities		35.00	

Fig. 4.10. Edit automatic sets to update them.

Hands-On Hints

Recalling Automatic Transaction Sets

Apple II, II+, and IIe

In the Account Selection Menu, first specify the Base Account (the Account you use to write checks). Find the number of the automatic set by pressing the D key repeatedly. Sets are numbered in order of their creation and are labeled `old`. To examine the first transactions in a set, ensure that you have the correct set by selecting `List Set (Option E)`. When you proceed to the entry screen, the automatic set reappears. The set is ready for you to update and reactivate.

Apple IIc

In the Enter Transactions Menu, first specify the Base Account (the Account you use to write checks). Find the number of the automatic set by pressing the E key repeatedly. Sets are numbered in order of their creation and are labeled `old`. Use `Option E`, `List Set` to examine the first transactions in the set and see whether the set is the one you want. When you proceed to the entry screen, the automatic set reappears. The set is ready for you to update and reactivate.

Releasing Automatic Sets

When you have 25 automatic sets and want to add another, you must first sacrifice an old set. To sacrifice an old set, Macintosh users must select Release Automatic Set from the Maintenance Menu. The dialog box that appears lets you specify which set to discard (fig. 4.11). Releasing an automatic set does not delete transactions from your file. That set will simply not reappear on command. In other configurations, use Release Set in the Account Selection Menu.

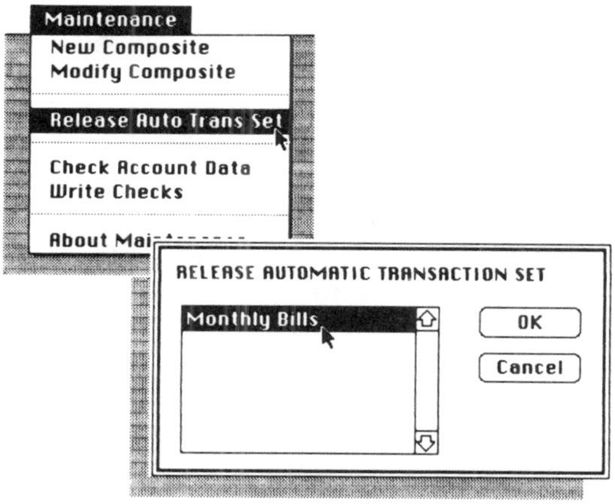

Fig. 4.11. Use the Release Set *option to select which set to discard.*

Printing Checks

As you pay bills, you can print checks directly from Dollars and Sense records. You need the right printer, and your program must be adjusted to suit the printer. Checks must be designed for use in your printer.

The Write Checks option is available from the Macintosh Maintenance Menu (fig. 4.12), or can be set up as an automatic sequence after entering transactions.

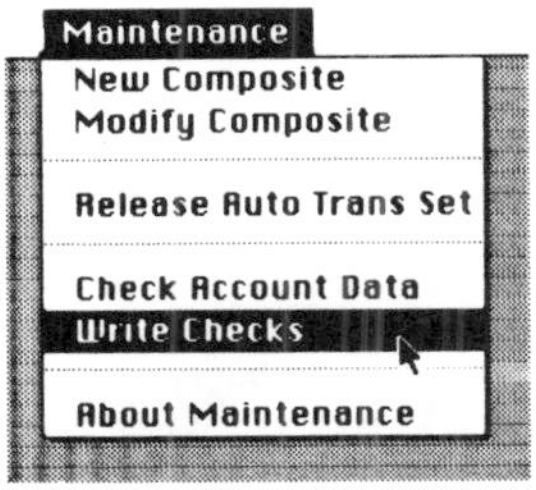

Fig. 4.12. The Macintosh Write Checks *option.*

You can select the account on which checks will be written and specify date and check ranges. You can also choose to see each check displayed before printing (fig. 4.13).

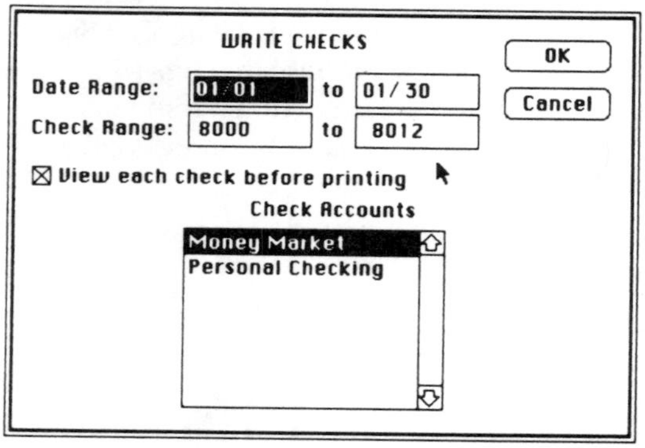

Fig. 4.13. Select the account, number, and date range.

When you choose to display a check before printing, a facsimile check that is already filled out appears in the window (fig. 4.14). All transactions in the requested ranges will appear in sequence. You may need to use Skip to find those checks you intend to print. You may choose to add the payee's address, and a reminder of what the check is for. The address is positioned to be visible through windowed envelopes.

Click the Print box for each check to be printed. Printing may not begin right away because print commands are stored on file first, and printing occurs intermittently. Continue to click Print for each check. When you have finished, click Quit. Printing will continue until all the checks are printed.

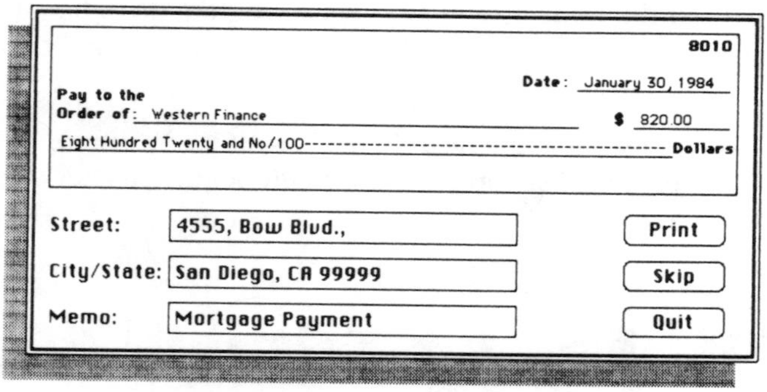

Fig. 4.14. A facsimile check in the Macintosh window.

The Account Selection Menus in most computers have an option for setting up check writing as an automatic sequence after new transactions have been saved.

Hands-On Hints

Printing Checks

Apple II, II+, and IIe

Option J of the Main Menu first displays the Check Writer Menu, which has name, bank, and code identifiers to help verify that you are printing from the proper account.

The screen can list as many as 12 CHECK Accounts as options. When you select an Account, its details are displayed on the right side of the screen. You must specify the date and number ranges for checks. You can also have a test character printed to help you align the checks in the printer.

When you proceed from the Check Writer Menu, the `Checks` screen appears. This screen shows details of the next check—number, date, title, and amount. You now have four choices: you can print the check, you can skip the check, you can write more information on the check, or you can print the check and all remaining checks.

Apple IIc

Option J of the Main Menu first displays the Check Writer Menu, which has name, bank, and code identifiers to help verify that you are printing from the proper account.

With Option A, and by searching and scrolling, find the Account for which checks are to be printed. You can also press Apple-A for a list of Account names, then press Return to select an Account.

When you select an Account, its details are displayed on the right side of the screen. You must specify the date and number ranges for checks. You can also have a test check printed, to help you align checks in the printer.

When you proceed from the Check Writer Menu, the `Checks` screen appears. This screen shows details of the next check. You now have four choices: you can print the check, you can skip the check, you can write more information on the check, or you can print the check and all remaining checks.

Reconciling Bank Statements

If you make mistakes while recording transactions in Dollars and Sense, you cannot expect your Accounts to balance or your graphs and reports to reflect reality. All computer fanciers know that "GIGO," the acronym for a principle that applies to data processing, means "Garbage In, Garbage Out." What you get out of a program is only as good as what you put into the program. Dollars and Sense can often alert you if the data you enter is demonstrably wrong but certain mistakes are not obvious.

Your opportunity to identify such mistakes recurs each month as you reconcile your bank statement. Dollars and Sense may not make reconciliation pleasant, but if you find the procedure an ordeal, the program should make reconciliation less painful.

You use three different windows for complete reconciliation: one to specify which transactions to display, another to check off cleared transactions, and a third to confirm that your Dollars and Sense records agree (or do not agree) with the bank's records. The process is initiated by the Select Menu option (fig. 4.15).

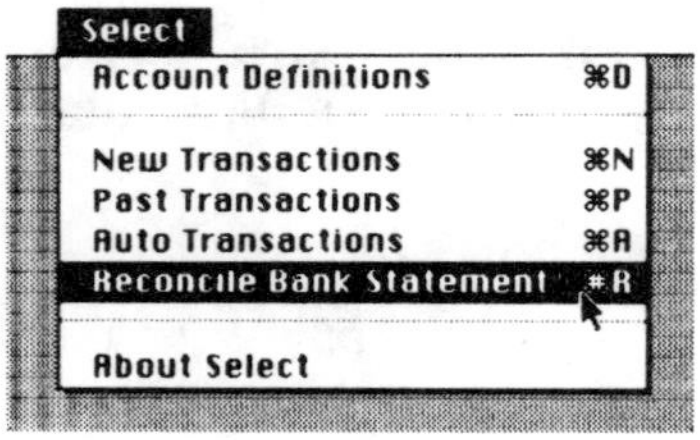

Fig. 4.15. Reconciliation is initiated by a Select Menu option.

Selecting Transactions

You must first indicate which CHECK Account is to be reconciled. Then by taking advantage of the Menu's Transaction Query Criteria options, you can be specific about which transactions you want to see. Macintosh users recall transactions with the Reconciliation Query box (fig. 4.16). You can set a date and check number range. Unless you do so, the entire range of up to 90 transactions in the Base Account will appear. Your bank statement will help you define the beginning and ending dates and numbers. You can also set a number range. Unless you do, all the numbered checks will appear. If you want to see only deposits and miscellaneous transactions, make the first number greater than the last. Transactions can be made to appear in date or check order. You also have the choice of calling for all transactions in the range or for uncleared transactions only.

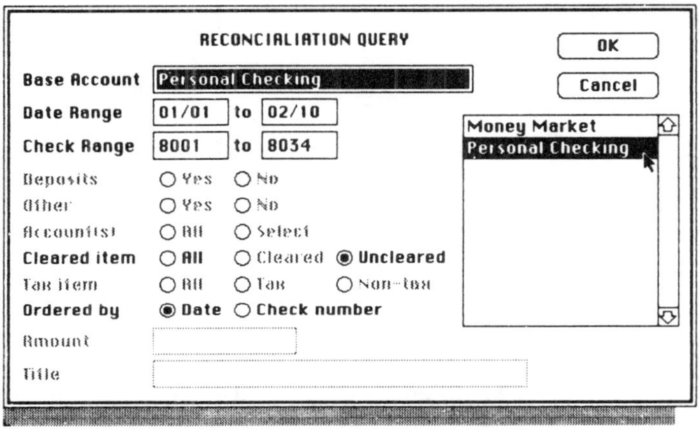

Fig. 4.16. The Macintosh RECONCILIATION QUERY box.

When you proceed from this window, the requested transactions are displayed for reconciliation. You can recall only 90 transactions at a time. If there are more than 90, simply continue the reconciliation process.

The Reconciliation Window

The window for reconciling transactions is almost a replica of the check entry window but operates differently (fig. 4.17). Specified transactions are displayed in the order you request.

The Account's balance, at the screen's upper right, is updated by each transaction you clear and is a record of the bank's version of your financial activity.

The first transaction is automatically highlighted by the `Clear` column at far left. As you compare the bank statement with your own records, mark each cleared transaction with *C* (Macintosh users do so by clicking the `Yes` button) as the cursor moves vertically down the `Clear` column. If you make a mistake, you can easily go back and change a check's cleared status.

Use the `void` button to cancel a check or deposit. In other systems, you would select the letter `V` when the cursor is in the `CHECK #` field.

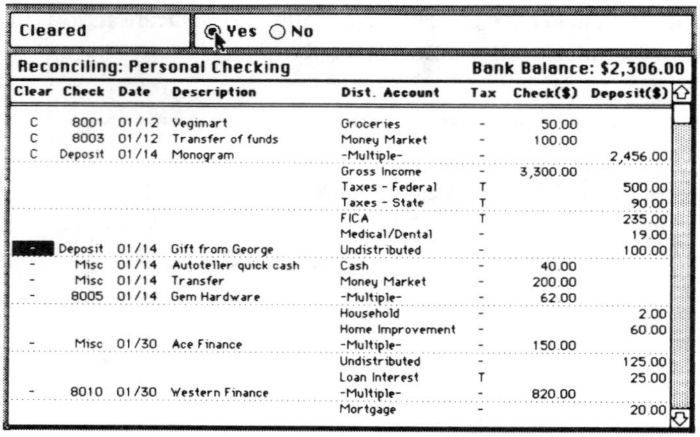

Cleared ◉ Yes ○ No

Reconciling: Personal Checking — Bank Balance: $2,306.00

Clear	Check	Date	Description	Dist. Account	Tax	Check($)	Deposit($)
C	8001	01/12	Vegimart	Groceries	-	50.00	
C	8003	01/12	Transfer of funds	Money Market	-	100.00	
C	Deposit	01/14	Monogram	-Multiple-	-		2,456.00
				Gross Income	-	3,300.00	
				Taxes - Federal	T		500.00
				Taxes - State	T		90.00
				FICA	T		235.00
				Medical/Dental	-		19.00
	Deposit	01/14	Gift from George	Undistributed	-		100.00
-	Misc	01/14	Autoteller quick cash	Cash	-	40.00	
-	Misc	01/14	Transfer	Money Market	-	200.00	
-	8005	01/14	Gem Hardware	-Multiple-	-	62.00	
				Household	-		2.00
				Home Improvement	-		60.00
-	Misc	01/30	Ace Finance	-Multiple-	-	150.00	
				Undistributed	-		125.00
				Loan Interest	T		25.00
-	8010	01/30	Western Finance	-Multiple-	-	820.00	
				Mortgage	-		20.00

Fig. 4.17. Clear transactions in the reconciliation window.

You may find that your Dollars and Sense record of an amount differs occasionally from the bank's record. Should this happen, check other documentary evidence such as a cancelled check or a deposit receipt. You can easily edit your mistake in this screen. Make a note of any error clearly made by the bank. You can bring errors to the bank's attention after you finish reconciling the statement.

Hands-On Hints

Clearing Transactions

Apple II, II+, and IIe

Press the C key to clear a check that agrees with the bank statement. If you change your mind, go back and press the U key to "unclear" a check. Press Alt-Q or the Q key to quit and save.

Apple IIc

Press the C key to clear a check that agrees with the bank statement. If you change your mind about a check, go back and press the U key to "unclear" that check. Press Apple-S or click `Save` to save the transactions.

The Reconciliation Status

When you have entered each check's cleared status and saved, the reconciliation status window is displayed (fig. 4.18). The reconciliation status window shows a breakdown of all checks, deposits, and miscellaneous transactions that have been cleared as well as those that have yet to be cleared. Be sure to record any additional charges or interest mentioned on the bank statement. These amounts will be distributed to the mandatory Check Charges and Check Interest Accounts.

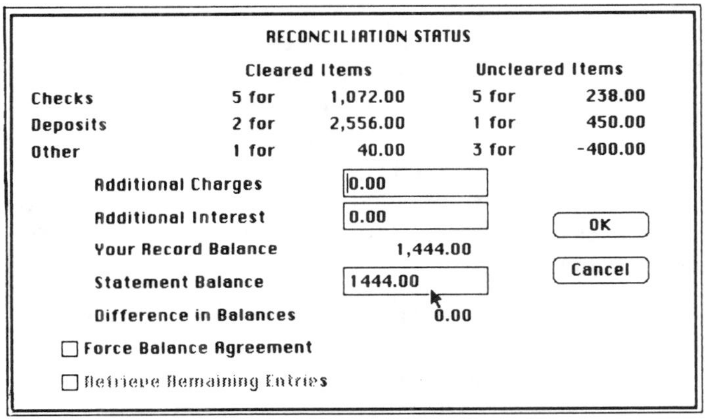

Fig. 4.18. The reconciliation status window.

Both the balance on the bank statement and the balance according to your records are displayed as well as any discrepancy that may exist between them. The size of a discrepancy will govern what you do next. Ordinarily, differences are small. You can update your records to agree with the bank's by using the `Force Balance Agreement` option in the reconciliation status window.

If the difference is large, you can quit this screen and run the reconciliation process again to locate any errors. If you find no mistakes, review last month's reconciliation to see whether the problem started at that time. Once you are sure that your records are in order, you can challenge the bank. You will have a fair chance of success if you have run Dollars and Sense properly.

When you have more than 90 transactions to reconcile, the reconciliation status window has an option to display the remaining transactions.

Unreconciled checks can be included in next month's session. Be sure to keep canceled checks for tax purposes.

Managing Credit and Debit Cards

Although bank credit cards initially were granted only to the wealthiest customers, anyone with a good credit history is eligible today. Millions of us carry some kind of "plastic money" in our wallets or purses.

Travel and entertainment cards such as Carte Blanche, Diners Club, and the American Express card are aimed primarily at people who can either afford such luxuries or who are on expense accounts. The advantage of these cards is that they have a high line of credit. A disadvantage may be that payment in full is expected within 20 to 30 days of receipt of the bill. Some travel and entertainment premium cards charge an annual fee of as much as $250. Prestige and enhanced buying power can be expensive.

Credit cards can be a convenient method of payment. They are particularly useful for business transactions because, unlike canceled checks, cardholder copies are accepted as proof of purchase by the IRS.

Businesses around the world accept VISA and MasterCard, the most popular bank credit cards. Bank cards generally require a minimum monthly payment of $10 to $30, but allow up to 36 months for repayment (with interest). Keeping a large balance in a credit card account can be ruinous. Annual interest rates run as high as 22 percent.

Bank cards are a source of small, interest-free, short-term loans to those who pay bills in full and on time. Therefore, be sure to keep a close eye on your credit card expenditures, and pay the bill promptly if you can. Dollars and Sense can help you, particularly if you enter your purchases soon after you make them.

Accounts for Credit Card Management

You need one LIABILITY Account for each card, as well as an appropriate EXPENSE Account to record finance charges. Your Account list should include categories for purchases that you may make with a credit card (fig. 4.19). If you use a card primarily for business transactions, you will find that business EXPENSE Accounts help keep your records in order.

Fig. 4.19. Credit card management: typical list of Accounts.

Account Definitions

Number	Account Name	Type	Monthly Budget	Starting Balance
100	Personal Checking	Check	0.00	0.00
300	MasterCard	Liability	0.00	0.00
310	VISA	Liability	0.00	0.00
320	American Express	Liability	0.00	0.00
500	Auto Expenses	Expense	0.00	0.00
510	Bus. Entertainment	Expense	0.00	0.00
520	Pers. Entertainment	Expense	0.00	0.00
530	Bus. Expenses	Expense	0.00	0.00
540	Credit Card Charges	Expense	0.00	0.00
550	Clothing	Expense	0.00	

Recording Purchases

Your spending patterns will probably determine which method you choose to record credit card purchases. The ideal method is to record each credit card transaction shortly after the transaction occurs, using your cardholder copy as a reference. There are two advantages to this approach. You can specify what you have paid for, and with a transaction report, you can also predict your liability before a bill arrives.

You may prefer to wait for the statement, then copy the transactions into your records. You need do this only once a month, but descriptions of transactions may be vague, and you will have little time to decide how to pay the bill.

To record credit card purchases, designate a Credit Card Account as the Base Account. You will notice that the entry screen for a LIABILITY Account differs from the entry screen for CHECK Accounts (fig. 4.20). In a LIABILITY entry screen, the last two columns record `Purchases` and `Payments` instead of `Checks(&)` and `Deposits($)`. Another significant difference is that the balance displays not how much credit you have but how much you owe the credit card company.

Figure 4.20 shows how to record a simple credit card transaction. This transaction increases by $18.00 the amount owed to VISA. The Account name, `VISA`, and the date are initially supplied by default. The description in this case is the name of the payee. The purchase, an oil change for a private car on a personal trip, is distributed to the Auto Expenses Account but not flagged with `T`.

Fig. 4.20. A simple credit card transaction.

Entering: VISA

Base Account	Date	Description	Dist. Account	Tax	Purchase	Payment
VISA	02/12	Lou's Shell , oil change	Auto Expenses	-	18.00	

You often need to make a multiple distribution (fig. 4.21). The $25 VISA payment to Officeland includes both business stationary and a lamp for the house. You must split the amount between different Accounts and flag the business-related portion of the transaction with T. This transaction increases the balances of three Accounts simultaneously.

Entering: VISA

Base Account	Date	Description	Dist. Account	Tax	Purchase	Payment
VISA	02/12	Officeland: Paper, lamp.	-Multiple-	-	25.00	
			Bus. Misc. Expens	T		10.00
			Furniture	-		15.00

Fig. 4.21. Multiple distribution of a credit card transaction.

Entering Transactions into Other LIABILITY Accounts

When you enter transactions, all your credit card Accounts can be accessed from the same screen (fig. 4.22). You can switch from one LIABILITY Account to another just by writing the Account name in the first column.

Entering: VISA

Base Account	Date	Description	Dist. Account	Tax	Purchase	Payment
VISA	02/12	Officeland: Paper, lamp.	-Multiple-	-	25.00	
			Bus. Misc. Expens	T		10.00
			Furniture	-		15.00
American Express	02/20	Lunch with Bill	Bus. Entertainment	T	46.00	
VISA	02/29	Taxi to LAX	Bus. Misc. Expens	T	30.00	

Fig. 4.22. Access all credit card Accounts with one screen.

Paying Your Credit Card Bill

To pay the credit card company, start with a CHECK Base Account. Figure 4.23 shows how to distribute the amount. This distribution reduces your liability but increases the balance of an EXPENSE Account that indicates finance charges.

Entering: Personal Checking

Clear	Check	Date	Description	Dist. Account	Tax	Check($)	Deposit($)
-	8030	02/10	VISA payment	-Multiple-	-	65.00	
				VISA	-		60.00
				Credit Card Charge	T		5.00

Fig. 4.23. Distribution of a credit card payment.

Note that although the payment has actually reduced your VISA balance by $65, your VISA Account shows a reduction of only $60. The remaining $5 has gone to an EXPENSE Account for finance charges. This program limitation simply means that your estimate of what you owe VISA can be slightly higher than the amount VISA bills you. The discrepancy may never disappear, but the difference need never be greater than the amount of the finance charge on your latest statement.

The Debit Card

Debit cards are a recent innovation. These cards, issued by banks, look like credit cards. There is, however, a significant difference between the two. Credit card bills arrive monthly, and you decide when to pay them. Debit cards, on the other hand, mean virtually instant payment. When you use a debit card, your bank account is debited automatically as soon as the bank learns of the transaction. Debit card owners need to create an appropriate LIABILITY Account and must begin to keep exceptionally careful records, entering amounts in Dollars and Sense as soon as possible after using the card.

Charge and Gas Cards

The procedures for tracking credit card purchases apply equally well to charge cards issued by big stores and oil companies. Make sure you have a LIABILITY Account for each card. Be sure to distribute gas card purchases that apply to business to the correct business EXPENSE Account.

Overdraft Protection

More and more banks now offer overdraft protection accounts, automatic liabilities that spring into action whenever your checking account is overdrawn. Overdraft protection is a convenient way to take out small short-term loans. A loan is created, and the shortfall is siphoned automatically from the loan account to checking account. Interest and finance charges vary from bank to bank, as does the maximum amount of protection. An overdraft protection account often costs less to use than a conventional passbook loan. As always, you must watch how much you borrow to avoid excess finance charges and to know when your protection is about to run out.

Create a LIABILITY Account for your overdraft protection account. Give the Account a number in the 300s to group the Account with your other LIABILITY Accounts. Initially, there is no need for either a starting balance or a monthly budget. You can budget a repayment schedule later if you decide to pay off the account.

Whenever you see that the CHECK Account linked to your overdraft account has gone into the red, you can restore the Account's balance (fig. 4.24).

Entering: Personal Checking

Clear	Check	Date	Description	Dist. Account	Tax	Check($)	Deposit($)
-	Deposit	02/15	Rebalance checking	Autobalance	-		230.00

Fig. 4.24. Balancing your overdraft protection Account.

The balance of the distribution Account, a LIABILITY Account, is increased by the amount of the transfer. Use a transaction report to find out how much you owe your protection account.

Although the bank automatically transfers money from protection account to checking account, with most banks the transfer is a one-way transaction. Repayment is your responsibility. Finance charges and interest must be accounted for separately, the same as with credit cards. A payment to an overdraft protection account might look like figure 4.25.

Entering: Personal Checking

Clear	Check	Date	Description	Dist. Account	Tax	Check($)	Deposit($)
-	8035	02/20	Repay Autobalance	-Multiple-	-	230.00	
				Autobalance	-		225.00
				Loan Interest	T		5.00

Fig. 4.25. Distribution of an overdraft protection payment.

Budget Control

Good budgeting requires a blend of rigidity and flexibility. Establish the habit of checking your budgets monthly. Discipline yourself to follow a budget, but be flexible enough to change a budget that seems impractical.

If your grocery budget seems inadequate, for example, take the time to analyze exactly what you buy at the supermarket. Some of your purchases may be extravagant, but if you know that the grocery bill is as low as possible, you should change the budget. You may find money available in other areas as you check your other budgets.

A cash flow report can show you exactly how your spending compares with your budgets. Use a Report Menu option to initiate a cash flow report. You can then select a range for the report from the Cash Flow dialog box.

The cash flow report in figure 4.26 clearly shows that the grocery budget is too low while other budgets are too high. Knowing this, the owner of these records can go back to the Account definitions screen and adjust the budgets. This back and forth activity, inevitable when you first use Dollars and Sense, gives you valuable insight into what your money is really doing.

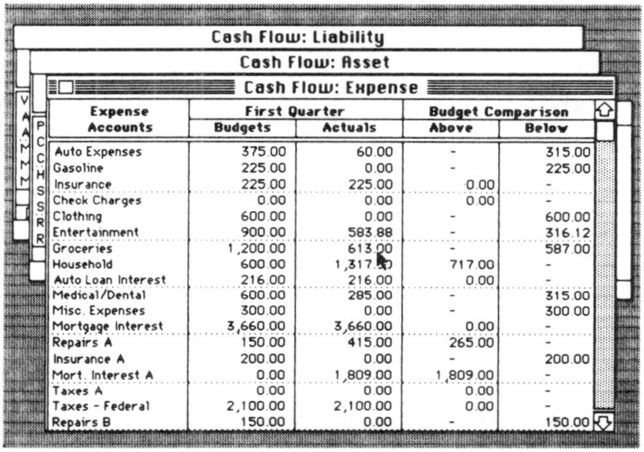

Expense Accounts	First Quarter Budgets	First Quarter Actuals	Budget Comparison Above	Budget Comparison Below
Auto Expenses	375.00	60.00	-	315.00
Gasoline	225.00	0.00	-	225.00
Insurance	225.00	225.00	0.00	-
Check Charges	0.00	0.00	0.00	-
Clothing	600.00	0.00	-	600.00
Entertainment	900.00	583.88	-	316.12
Groceries	1,200.00	613.00	-	587.00
Household	600.00	1,317.[illegible]0	717.00	-
Auto Loan Interest	216.00	216.00	0.00	-
Medical/Dental	600.00	285.00	-	315.00
Misc. Expenses	300.00	0.00	-	300.00
Mortgage Interest	3,660.00	3,660.00	0.00	-
Repairs A	150.00	415.00	265.00	-
Insurance A	200.00	0.00	-	200.00
Mort. Interest A	0.00	1,809.00	1,809.00	-
Taxes A	0.00	0.00	0.00	-
Taxes - Federal	2,100.00	2,100.00	0.00	-
Repairs B	150.00	0.00	-	150.00

Fig. 4.26. A Cash Flow Report.

Hands-On Hints

Cash Flow Reports

Cash Flow reports show the distribution of income. Note that amounts shown in `Cash Flow: Asset` and `Cash Flow: Liability` are the amounts spent on the Accounts, *not* their current balances.

The Apple Family

Select Option G, `Prepare Reports`, from the Main Menu. For a Cash Flow report, choose Option G from the Reports Menu. The Cash Flow Menu appears, giving you an opportunity to choose different kinds of reports. For a summary of monthly balances in a specific Account, write the Account name at `H` and proceed.

Budget Comparisons with Composite Graphs

The information that Dollars and Sense supplies in reports can also be presented in graphs, thanks to the program's powerful graph-making capability. You can compare a single Account or group of Accounts with any other Accounts, thereby casting light on any aspect of your finances. You can show where major expenditures occur, the relative importance of sources of income, and the relationship between income and expenses.

Select an Actuals vs. Budgets graph from the Graph Menu to see how your actual expenses compare with the budgets you set up. The new window that appears enables you to choose which type of Accounts to examine (fig. 4.27). Notice that these Account types appear within quotation marks. This indicates that they are composite Accounts or groups of Accounts already put together in a way that can be expressed graphically. Dollars and Sense provides four ready-made composite Accounts: "ASSETS," "LIABILITIES," "INCOMES," and "EXPENSES."

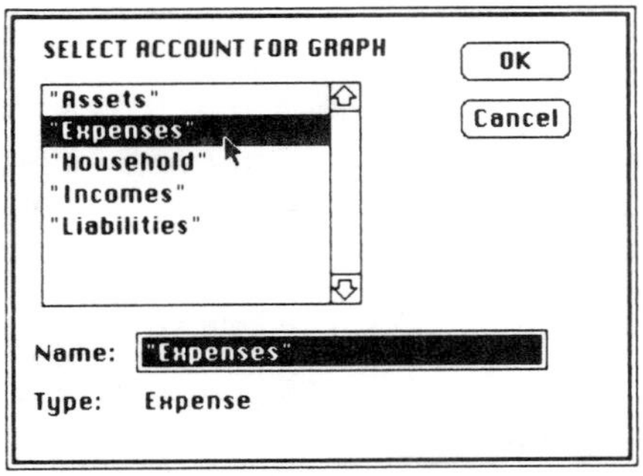

Fig. 4.27. Selecting a Composite Account for Graphical Comparisons.

By choosing "Expenses" and OK-ing the box, you will see the Actual vs Budget for "Expenses" graph (fig. 4.28). This graph, often several pages long, compares in detail the actual total of each EXPENSE Account with its budget. You can see at a glance which budgets are too low and which are too high. As with the cash flow report, you can use this information to curb your spending or rewrite your budgets.

You can create composite Accounts for a variety of studies. If you own two rental properties, for example, you can create a composite Account to compare such different aspects as the costs of interest and upkeep.

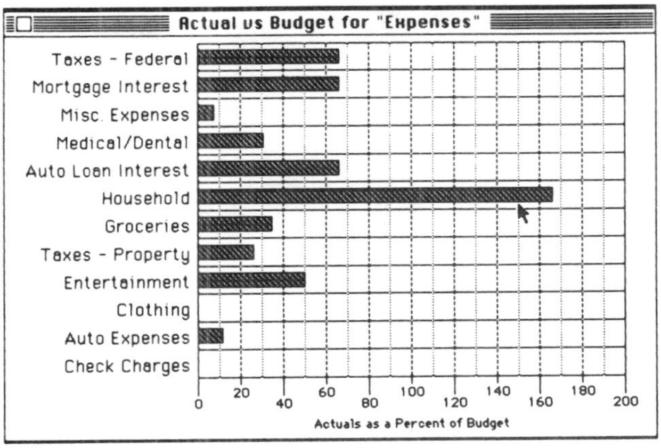

Fig. 4.28. The Actual vs. Budget graph for "Expenses."

Your composite Account will include all EXPENSE Accounts related to the two rentals. The Macintosh define new composite Account window (fig. 4.29), which appears when you select `New Composite` from the Maintenance Menu, lets you specify Accounts. Composite Accounts must also be given a name, always in quotation marks, that identifies them. In this case, the name can be "Rental Study."

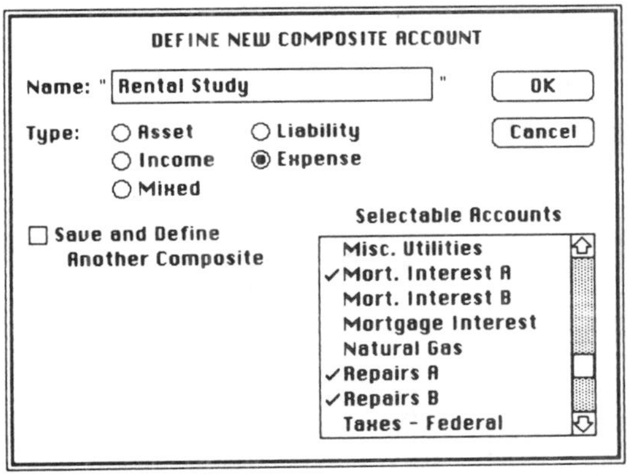

Fig. 4.29. Selecting the Accounts that will make up the new Composite Account.

The new composite Account can now be used for an `Actual Contribution to Totals` graph. This time the name of the new Account appears in the selection window (fig. 4.30).

This pie graph first compares actual expenditures (fig. 4.31) and then does the same for the budgets (fig. 4.32).

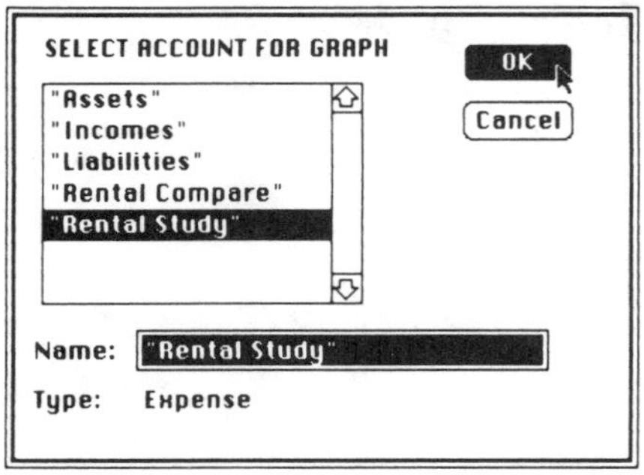

Fig. 4.30. Selecting an Account for a graph.

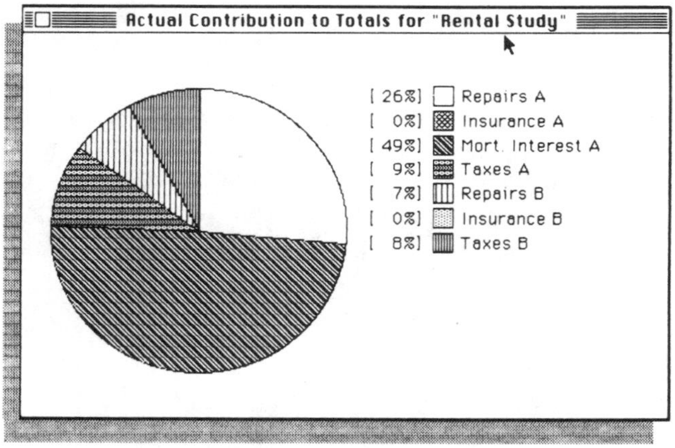

Fig. 4.31. Actual Contribution to Totals.

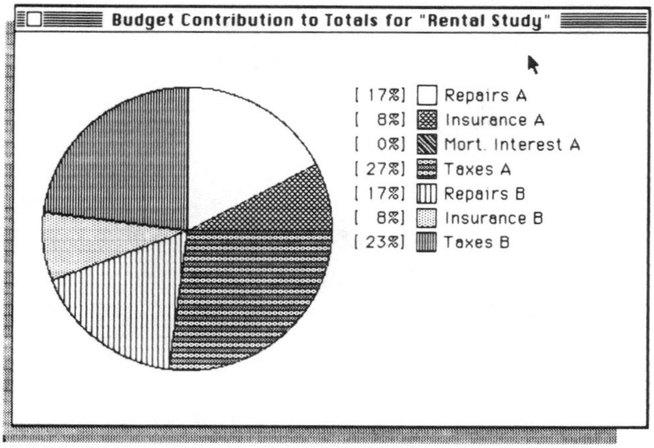

Fig. 4.32. Budget comparisons for the "Rental Study."

5 Annual Sessions

Companies and corporations—large and small—issue annual reports to indicate how successful their business activities were during the past year and to forecast what can be expected during the coming year. Your personal annual report should be of paramount interest to you. At least once a year, imagine that you are president of your own company and do your best to report objectively what happened to your money during the past year. Such an exercise will help you plan strategies to avoid past mistakes and capitalize on your successes.

Most of us, of course, are required by law to submit an annual report to the Internal Revenue Service. Consistent use of Dollars and Sense will keep your finger on the pulse of your financial circulation so that the annual tax ritual will produce few surprises.

Cash-Flow Problems

Large businesses, small businesses, rich people, poor people—all have cash-flow problems at times. Your overall annual budget may balance perfectly and look great on paper, but there will always be times when your expenses and liabilities tower threateningly over your income.

Self-employed persons, whose incomes can vary dramatically from year to year, are particularly vulnerable to cash-flow problems. Failing to account for estimated tax can put a small business or free-lance practice out of action. A good year generates a large estimated tax bill for the following year, but if the following year is lean, the tax bite can be ruinous.

Demoralizing, disabling cash-flow problems can be avoided with little more than information and planning. Keep four basic steps in mind as you plan your strategy:

1. Identify large and irregular, but predictable, expenses.
2. Identify the source of income that will be used to pay these expenses.
3. Set a savings goal and schedule for each expense.
4. Save. Keep track of progress until you attain a goal, then pay the bill.

Budget Reports

You took the first step in identifying where and when cash flow problems may arise and how big they may be when you set up your variable budgets. A graph can give you a clear picture of irregular but predictable expenses. An even more exact picture comes from a monthly budget report (fig. 5.1).

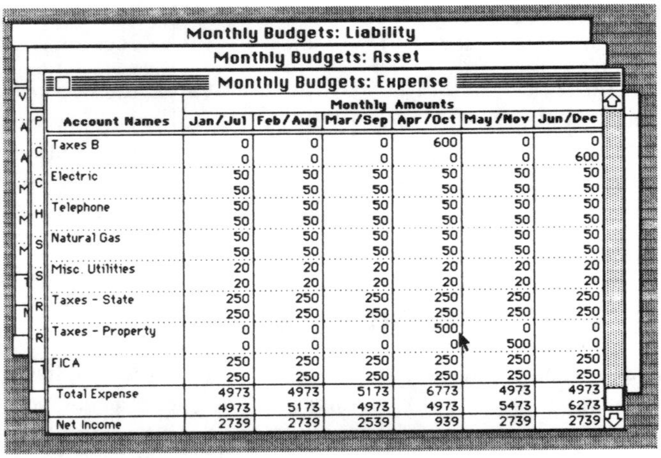
Monthly Budgets: Liability
Monthly Budgets: Asset
Monthly Budgets: Expense

Account Names	Monthly Amounts Jan/Jul	Feb/Aug	Mar/Sep	Apr/Oct	May/Nov	Jun/Dec
Taxes B	0	0	0	600	0	0
	0	0	0	0	0	600
Electric	50	50	50	50	50	50
	50	50	50	50	50	50
Telephone	50	50	50	50	50	50
	50	50	50	50	50	50
Natural Gas	50	50	50	50	50	50
	50	50	50	50	50	50
Misc. Utilities	20	20	20	20	20	20
	20	20	20	20	20	20
Taxes - State	250	250	250	250	250	250
	250	250	250	250	250	250
Taxes - Property	0	0	0	500	0	0
	0	0	0	0	500	0
FICA	250	250	250	250	250	250
	250	250	250	250	250	250
Total Expense	4973	4973	5173	6773	4973	4973
	4973	5173	4973	4973	5473	6273
Net Income	2739	2739	2539	939	2739	2739

Fig. 5.1. A monthly budget totals report.

Working from such reports, you can predict probable cash flow problems well in advance. Suppose that you have a few major foreseeable liabilities in February, April, November, and December. These are months when property taxes and large insurance payments are due. Detailed reports for such Accounts as Taxes-Property, Insurance-Home, Insurance-Life, and Insurance-Car, can show you the exact amounts due. April is the cruelest month, with a total of $800 for property taxes and insurance.

The Money Market Account for Contingency Savings

The only way to ensure that you have enough cash to meet large, irregular bills is to save for them. To do so, you need a savings account from which funds can be drawn readily when needed. If you are satisfied with your existing savings account, you probably use the account to cover foreseeable large bills. Dollars and Sense can help you control both savings and disbursement.

If you intend to open a new savings account, you may want to consider one of many money market accounts currently available. Money market accounts earn more interest than passbook savings accounts, deposits are federally insured, and in most cases, you can withdraw money without advance notice. As you assess different types of savings accounts, keep three main criteria in mind:

1. Security. How safe will your money be?
2. Interest. How much will you earn?
3. Ease of access. How easily can you withdraw money when needed?

You may decide to open a money market account as a cash flow buffer account. Dollars and Sense designates this type of account as a CHECK Account (fig. 5.2).

Fig. 5.2. Starting a Money Market Account.

Account Definitions

In Use	Number	Account Name	Type	Monthly Budget	Starting Balance
	103	Money Market	Check	0.00	200.00

This Account is grouped, by its number, with existing CHECK Accounts, and its starting balance is the amount used to open the Account. Divide the total amount of your large foreseeable expenses by 12, to get an overall view of how much must be saved each month. You must also factor the date an expense is due into the way you save. Whether or not your savings are all in one Account, the money saved for predicted cash flow difficulties must be recorded separately.

Planning and Saving

Suppose that you begin in January to prepare for a heavy cash drain in April, the month that property tax and life insurance payments are due. You need a total of $800, and you decide to put money for both bills into the Money Market Account. With four months in which to save $800, you plan to save $50 a week. You can either write checks from your Personal Checking Account to the Money Market Account or set up a weekly or monthly automatic transfer to move the money into the Money Market Account. For the sake of illustration, check writing will be used in this example.

Because the contingency savings plan involves regular payments, you can set up your Money Market deposits as an automatic set. Recall the set either weekly or monthly, make necessary changes in dates and check numbers, and reactivate the set.

Dollars and Sense lets you record increases to a Money Market account while earmarking different amounts for different savings goals. The obvious method of writing a check in Personal Checking and distributing the check to Money Market has limited effectiveness in tracking funds earmarked for future expenditures.

To earmark funds, transfers are written as increases to the Money Market Account, rather than as checks in the Account that is the source of the money (fig. 5.3). Dollars and Sense automatically records the payment in Personal Checking. The transaction decreases the balance of the Personal Checking Account, and increases the Money Market fund by $25. You will see the wisdom of making savings the Base Account when we examine the method in more detail.

Entering: Money Market

Clear	Check	Date	Description	Dist. Account	Tax	Check($)	Deposit($)
-	Deposit	01/07	Property Tax saving	Personal Checking	-		25.00

Fig. 5.3. Money Market Account transfer.

When you write a check that covers savings for more than one purpose, record the transaction in the Money Market Account as more than one deposit.

For example, you write a check for $50 to the Money Market Account and intend for half of the amount to be saved for property tax and the other half for life insurance. By entering the transaction as increases to the Money Market Account, a record of two amounts with a description of their purpose is recorded in the Account. The Money Market Account has been increased by $50, and the Personal Checking Account has decreased accordingly. This appears to be two transactions, but actually only a single transaction, a transfer of $50 from one Account to another, has occurred (fig. 5.4). By splitting the transaction in this way, Dollars and Sense keeps a record of money earmarked for specific purposes while maintaining the integrity of the Account balance.

Entering: Money Market

Clear	Check	Date	Description	Dist. Account	Tax	Check($)	Deposit($)
-	Deposit	01/07	Taxes, Property	Personal Checking	T		25.00
-	Deposit	01/07	Insurance-Life	Personal Checking	-		25.00

Fig. 5.4. Money Market Account distribution.

Resist any temptation to make a split distribution of the deposit. By doing so, you would artificially decrease the balances of the distribution accounts.

The value of this method becomes clear when you need to know how much you have saved toward a particular expenditure. A week or so before a large bill becomes due, you can create a transaction report to see if the full amount is earmarked in your Money Market Account.

In the transaction report selection window, select Money Market as the Base Account. In the Title field, enter `proper` for all savings amounts to be found. (Entering `Taxes-Property` in full will not allow for variations in entry.) The transaction report will detail all funds allocated to property tax (fig. 5.5). If you are short on cash, you can take evasive action; but with the Dollars and Sense cash flow planning procedure, you should be well ahead of the game.

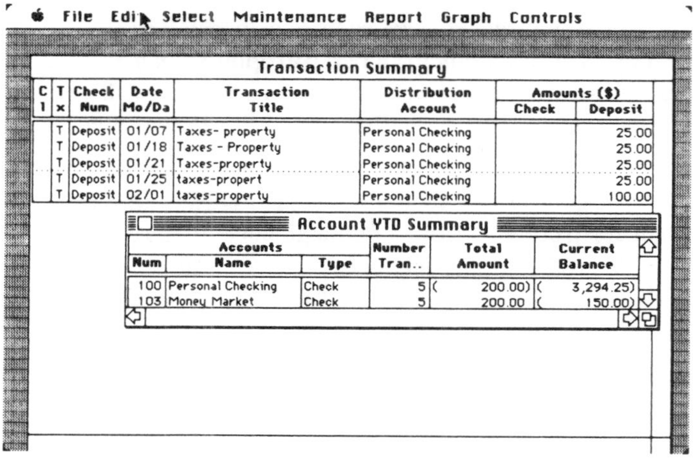

Fig. 5.5. A Transaction Summary and YTD Summary.

When the time comes to pay a large bill, you know that you have the money and exactly where the money came from. Make Money Market your Base Account, but this time record a decrease (fig. 5.6). Only at this point do you distribute to the Taxes-Property and Insurance-Life Accounts. The payments are recorded in these Accounts, while the Money Market Account balance is reduced by $800.

Entering: Money Market

Clear	Check	Date	Description	Dist. Account	Tax	Check($)	Deposit($)
-	3000	04/12	Ist Payment	Taxes - Property	T	500.00	
-	3001	04/12	LifeCo Inc	Insurance - Life	-	300.00	

Fig. 5.6. Distribution of payment from a Money Market Account.

Net Worth and Financial Disclosure Statements

The simplest definition of net worth is your assets minus your liabilities. In other words, net worth is the amount of money you would have if you paid all your debts.

The concept of net worth is vital to all money management. Check your net worth, the standard by which your financial health is measured, at least once a year. By so doing, you can monitor the development of your financial security and calculate the impact of proposed changes in income and expenditures on your future net worth.

Others will also be interested in your net worth, the bottom line of any financial disclosure statement. When you apply for a loan or start your own business, loan officers and prospective partners will want to see a financial disclosure statement that lists all factors that affect both your current and future net worth.

Many experts insist that calculating net worth is the indispensable starting point for gaining control of your finances. There is often a great deal of research and organizing to do before net worth can be calculated. You do that research and organization with Dollars and Sense simply by creating Accounts, budgets, starting balances, and by entering transactions. Dollars and Sense organizes the data you have entered, and provides necessary reports and graphs.

The Balance Sheet

The balance sheet report details your net worth by comparing your assets and liabilities. (The balances of your CHECK Accounts are also included in the balance sheet report.) The time period you specify determines whether the report is a year-to-date analysis, or whether the report will show details on an annual, quarterly, or monthly basis. Macintosh owners use the balance sheets option of the Report Menu and click appropriate buttons to select time periods for the report (fig. 5.7).

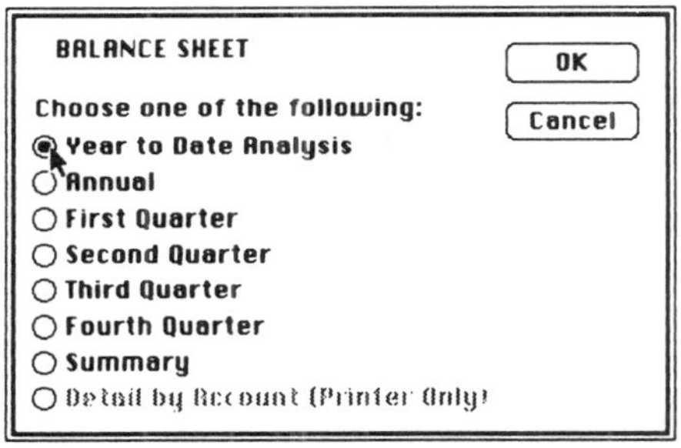

Fig. 5.7. Selecting a range for the balance sheet.

Hands-On Hints

Balance Sheets

The Apple Family

Select Option G, `Prepare Reports`, from the Main Menu. For a Balance Sheet, choose Option F from the Reports Menu. The Balance Sheet Menu appears, giving you an opportunity to specify a time period for the report.

Year-to-Date Analysis

The year-to-date balance sheet analysis shows what you are worth at the time you generate the report (fig. 5.8). This report contains an enormous amount of information. Used wisely, this report is an invaluable tool for planning as well as for assessing the current picture.

Analysis of Balance Sheet: Asset

Asset Accounts	Distribution (%)		Totals for Year		Act as % of Bdgt
	Budgets	Actuals	Budgets	Actuals	
Personal Checking	0.20	-0.40	1,250.00	(2,444.25)	-195.54
Money Market	0.03	-0.08	200.00	(500.00)	-250.00
Cash	0.01	0.01	50.00	50.00	100.00
Credit Union	0.93	0.04	5,873.00	250.00	4.26
Home	32.55	33.24	204,900.00	204,900.00	100.00
Stock Savings Plan	4.40	4.30	27,715.00	26,515.00	95.67
Stocks & Bonds	14.70	14.72	92,535.00	90,735.00	98.05
Rental A	24.94	25.47	157,000.00	157,000.00	100.00
Rental B	22.24	22.71	140,000.00	140,000.00	100.00
[Totals]	100.00	100.00	629,523.00	616,505.75	97.93

Analysis of Balance Sheet: Liability

Liability Accounts	Distribution (%)		Totals for Year		Act as % of Bdgt
	Budgets	Actuals	Budgets	Actuals	
Visa	0.04	-0.40	250.00	(2,466.00)	-986.40
American Express	0.07	-0.27	419.20	(1,692.16)	-403.66
Auto Loan	0.47	0.58	2,950.00	3,550.00	120.34
Mortgage	22.30	22.81	140,386.00	140,626.00	100.17
Mortgage A	16.90	17.29	106,397.00	106,598.00	100.19
Mortgage B	14.22	14.55	89,514.00	89,676.00	100.18
[Totals]	54.00	54.55	339,916.20	336,291.84	98.93
[Net]	46.00	45.45	289,606.80	280,213.91	96.76

Fig. 5.8. The balance sheet, showing a year-to-date analysis of net worth.

The first part of the report shows details of budgets and actual expenditure for each ASSET Account. For the purpose of reporting net worth, the balances of CHECK Accounts are treated as assets. Each column provides specific information:

1. `Budgets`. The first column of figures under the general subheading of `Distribution (%)` shows the percentage contributed by each Account budget to the total ASSET budget.

2. `Actuals`. The second column shows the actual percentage of contributions made by each Account to the actual value of total assets. Usually, figures in the `Budgets` and `Actuals` columns will not be identical, but a large difference between budgets and actuals in any category may indicate an unrealistic budget.

3. `Budgets`. The third column reports the budgeted values of your assets. (The third and fourth columns are under the general subheading of `Totals for Year`.)

4. `Actuals`. This column shows the actual balances of the ASSET Accounts. Negative figures in this column are a warning signal that your budget may not be working as planned.

5. `Act as % of Bdgt`. The fifth column shows to what extent your actuals coincide with your budgets. This column is another barometer of whether your budgets are realistic.

The next page of the balance sheet shows corresponding figures for your LIABILITY Accounts. Your actual net worth is displayed at the bottom of the fourth column.

Annual Balance Sheet

Your annual balance sheet shows both your net worth at year's end and how much your financial situation has improved or deteriorated in a year. Net worth should increase steadily year by year as you acquire assets and reduce liabilities.

Quarterly Balance Sheets

Quarterly balance sheets detail the activity of your ASSET Accounts compared to your LIABILITY Accounts. You need this feedback to see how your net worth evolves during the year.

Plotting the Trend of Your Net Worth

Ideally, net worth should increase year by year although not necessarily at a constant rate. If your balance sheets indicate that your net worth is shrinking, you must take positive action. Perhaps you should plan to change jobs or investigate different investments.

When the figures in reports do not give a clear impression of the trend of your net worth, use a Dollars and Sense graph. The Monthly Net Worth graph displays actual and budgeted net worth for each month of the year (fig. 5.9). A trend line shows whether your net worth is headed up or down.

Hands-On Hints

Net Worth Graphs

Net Worth graphs show actual and budgeted net worth with a trend line.

The Apple Family

Select Option H, `Prepare Graphs`, from the Main Menu. From the Graphs Menu, choose Option F. The `Monthly Net Worth` graph appears on screen and can also be printed.

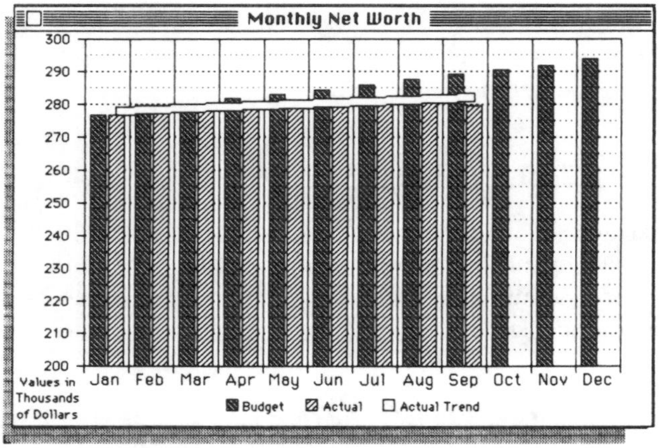

Fig. 5.9. The monthly net worth graph.

The Income Statement

Income statements are dynamic indicators of the relationship of your income to your expenses (fig. 5.10). Alone, a balance sheet that shows your current net worth is an inadequate indicator of your financial viability. A loan officer needs to know details of your past income and expenditures and how your income and expenditures are expected to develop. You can provide this information with a Dollars and Sense income statement.

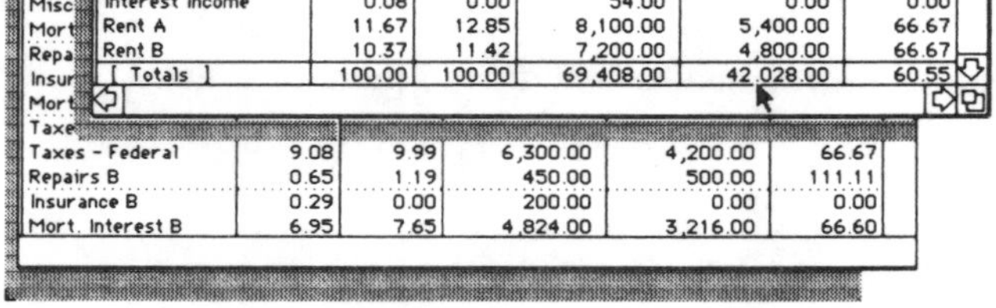

Analysis of Income Statement: Expense

Expense Accounts	Distribution (%) Budgets	Distribution (%) Actuals	Totals for Year Budgets	Totals for Year Actuals	Act as % of Bdgt
Auto Expenses	1.62	0.33	1,125.00	138.00	12.27
Gasoline	0.97	0.00	675.00	0.00	0.00
Insur[illegible]	[illegible]	[illegible]	[illegible]	[illegible]	[illegible]
Chec[illegible]					
Clot[illegible]					
Ente[illegible]					
Groc[illegible]					
Hous[illegible]					
Auto[illegible]					
Medi[illegible]					
Misc[illegible]					
Mort[illegible]					
Repa[illegible]					
Insur[illegible]					
Mort[illegible]					
Taxe[illegible]					
Taxes - Federal	9.08	9.99	6,300.00	4,200.00	66.67
Repairs B	0.65	1.19	450.00	500.00	111.11
Insurance B	0.29	0.00	200.00	0.00	0.00
Mort. Interest B	6.95	7.65	4,824.00	3,216.00	66.60

Analysis of Income Statement: Income

Income Accounts	Distribution (%) Budgets	Distribution (%) Actuals	Totals for Year Budgets	Totals for Year Actuals	Act as % of Bdgt
Check Interest	0.08	0.07	54.00	28.00	51.85
Dividends	9.08	0.00	6,300.00	0.00	0.00
Gross Income	68.72	75.66	47,700.00	31,800.00	66.67
Interest Income	0.08	0.00	54.00	0.00	0.00
Rent A	11.67	12.85	8,100.00	5,400.00	66.67
Rent B	10.37	11.42	7,200.00	4,800.00	66.67
[Totals]	100.00	100.00	69,408.00	42,028.00	60.55

Fig. 5.10. The year-to-date income statement.

Hands-On Hints

Income Statements

The Apple Family

Select Option G, `Prepare Reports`, from the Main Menu. For an Income Statement, choose Option E from the Reports Menu. The Income Statement Menu appears so that you can specify a time period for the statement.

In a monthly net income graph, Dollars and Sense provides a graphic presentation of your net income (fig. 5.11). The graph shows budgeted and actual income throughout the year. Budget irregularities result from extraordinary expenses in certain months. Because the trend line shows how net income increases or decreases, looking at this graph before the end of the year may give you a false picture of your income trend.

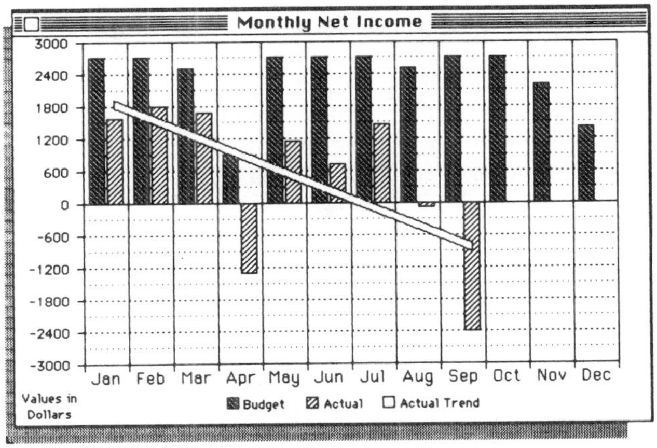

Fig. 5.11. The monthly net income graph.

Examined together, income statements and balance sheets provide a complete picture of your financial value. These reports and graphs provide information that can be used as the basis for all long-term financial decisions. These statements also provide the feedback you need to assess whether your financial plans are working out, to pinpoint problems, and to indicate a new course.

When you apply for a loan, you can give the loan officer printed copies of income statements, balance sheets, and even your net income and net worth graphs. More evidence may well be required, but the reports and graphs will save both of you time and work.

Household Inventories

You should keep an up-to-date list of your personal possessions and their value, an important part of your net worth, as a contribution to your assets. Inventories should be updated whenever you acquire a new item of value. Dollar amounts should be updated at least once every two years to show how your possessions are increasing or decreasing in value.

An inventory is important in the event of theft or fire, when insurance officers and policemen are grateful for a detailed list of possessions. Should you claim casualty losses, the IRS also needs detailed information.

Many insurance companies provide inventory forms that give some idea of what should be listed. Using an ASSET Account called Inventory or Household Goods as the Base Account, enter the items directly into Dollars and Sense (fig. 5.12).

Account Definitions

In Use	Number	Account Name	Type	Monthly Budget	Starting Balance
	208	Inventory	Asset	0.00	0.00

Fig. 5.12. An Inventory Account.

Establishing the value of individual items may be a problem. Appraisals for insurance or tax-loss claims must be highly detailed. Be sure to store safely such evidence as receipts and sales slips that can back up your appraisal.

You may want to consider a professional appraiser for valuable items. Appraisers usually charge from $20 to $100. Such charges can be money well spent because an insurance company will probably insist that the value of your property be assessed by a professional.

Appraisers use replacement cost and fair market value as criteria. Replacement cost is what you would have to pay to replace something. Fair market value is what a "willing buyer would pay a willing seller." Because dealers, antique dealers in particular, traditionally mark up items by at least 100 percent, the fair market value is roughly half the replacement cost.

Your inventory list should record replacement costs. Not only will you have a clear view of your net worth, but also an accurate assessment if your insurance is for replacement costs.

Fair market value is important when you donate property and want to claim a noncash contribution as a tax deduction. Fair market value is also important during divorce and estate settlements.

A printed copy of your inventory, receipts, and your written appraisals will provide necessary evidence if you ever have a claim. These documents should be kept by your lawyer or in a safe-deposit box.

When you create your Dollars and Sense Inventory Account, make the description as concise as possible, and always include serial numbers. Be sure to "shift" amounts so that the amounts will be recorded in the INCREASE column. Your Inventory Account could look like figure 5.13. Flag all business property with T. In case of fire or theft, a report of business losses can help in your claim from the IRS.

Entering: Inventory — Balance: $8,000.00

Base Account	Date	Description	Dist. Account	Tax	Decrease	Increase
Inventory	01/01	Queen Anne Table	Undistributed	-		3,500.00
Inventory	01/01	TV TSH123345	Undistributed	-		400.00
Inventory	01/01	Watercolor by Lear	Undistributed	-		1,300.00
Inventory	01/01	Whirlpool dishwasher 34...	Undistributed	-		350.00
Inventory	01/01	Encyclopædia Britannica	Undistributed	-		650.00
Inventory	01/01	Gibson A50 Mandolin	Undistributed	-		800.00
Inventory	01/01	Nikon SLR450098	Undistributed	T		1,000.00

Fig. 5.13. Sample Household Inventory Account.

Figure 5.14 shows how to record the purchase of a new item for your home. The transaction shows up automatically in the Inventory Account, and you can edit the description in the Account's edit transactions screen. If your purchase was a "steal," you can give the item a higher estimated value.

Entering: Personal Checking

Clear	Check	Date	Description	Dist. Account	Tax	Check($)	Deposit($)
-	8133	05/11	Art West Inc. Lear Pic.	Inventory	-	350.00	

Fig. 5.14. Record addition to your Inventory Account.

When you liquidate an asset, edit the inventory record by distributing the item to the CHECK Account that receives the money (fig. 5.15). Distribute a cash sale to the Cash on Hand Account. Shift the amount from the Increase to the Decrease column and change the date to the date of sale.

Editing: Inventory — **Balance: $8,500.00**

Base Account	Date	Description	Dist. Account	Tax	Decrease	Increase
Inventory	01/01	Queen Anne Table	Undistributed	-		3,500.00
Inventory	01/01	TV TSH123345	Undistributed	-		400.00
Inventory	01/01	Watercolor by Lear	Undistributed	-		1,300.00
Inventory	01/01	Whirlpool dishwasher 34	Undistributed	-		350.00
Inventory	01/01	Encyclopædia Britannica	Undistributed	-		650.00
Inventory	01/01	Gibson A50 Mandolin	Undistributed	-		800.00
Inventory	01/01	Nikon SLR450098	Undistributed	T		1,000.00
Inventory	05/11	Pink Dawn, wtrclr, Lear	Personal Checking	-		500.00

Fig. 5.15. Sale of asset increases CHECK Account.

The transaction shown in figure 5.16 neatly decreases your Inventory Account while increasing the balance of your CHECK Account.

Editing: Inventory — **Balance: $6,900.00**

Base Account	Date	Description	Dist. Account	Tax	Decrease	Increase
Inventory	01/01	Queen Anne Table	Undistributed	-		3,500.00
Inventory	01/01	TV TSH123345	Undistributed	-		400.00
Inventory	01/01	Watercolor by Lear	Undistributed	-		1,300.00
Inventory	01/01	Whirlpool dishwasher 34...	Undistributed	-		350.00
Inventory	01/01	Encyclopædia Britannica	Undistributed	-		650.00
Inventory	03/11	Gibson A50 Mandolin	Undistributed	-	800.00	
Inventory	01/01	Nikon SLR450098	Undistributed	T		1,000.00
Inventory	05/11	Art West Inc. Lear Pic.	Personal Checking	-		500.00

Fig. 5.16. Sale of asset decreases Inventory Account.

The transaction, however, would not be as neat if the mandolin were sold for either more or less than its appraised value. If you sold the mandolin for $600, for example, and edited the transaction accordingly, the balance of the Account would be thrown off by $200. You must write a transaction to indicate the loss (fig. 5.17).

Editing: Inventory

Base Account	Date	Description	Dist. Account	Tax	Decrease	Increase
Inventory	03/11	Gibson A50 Mandolin	Personal Checking		600.00	
Inventory	03/11	Loss on Gibson	Undistributed		200.00	

Fig. 5.17. A transaction indicating a loss.

To avoid artificially depleting your inventory balance if you make a profit, be sure to write a transaction to reflect the profit (fig. 5.18).

Editing: Inventory

Base Account	Date	Description	Dist. Account	Tax	Decrease	Increase
Inventory	03/11	Gibson A50 Mandolin	Personal Checking		900.00	
Inventory	03/11	Profit on Gibson	Undistributed			100.00

Fig. 5.18. A transaction indicating a profit.

6
Dollars and Sense and Taxes

A full discussion of tax preparation is beyond the scope of this book. Even if there were enough room, some facts would be out of date by the time you open this book. The tax law changes so rapidly that there is no guarantee that even general principles will remain valid for long.

The Internal Revenue code has been revised, rewritten, and recodified each year since 1939. Despite periodic attempts at simplification, the tax code today is extremely complex.

Most income earners are required to pay federal income tax, but not even the IRS expects anyone to pay more than the legal minimum. We are at liberty to take advantage of all available loopholes, but given the complexity of the tax code, those loopholes can be difficult to identify.

To discover how to pay the least amount of income tax, you can either hire an expert or become one yourself. Experts are seldom cheap, but can save you money, especially if your tax picture is complicated. If you decide to do your own taxes, you will find all the information you need in the many excellent tax guides published each year. The money you spend on accountants or books is also tax deductible.

Dollars and Sense cannot prepare your taxes for you. The program can, however, quickly and efficiently supply all the figures needed to fill out your tax forms. Transaction reports can show the balances of all tax-related Accounts and transactions. In many cases these figures can be transferred without adjustment to your tax forms.

Another advantage of using the program is that your Dollars and Sense transaction reports can serve as an electronic diary. Legally, you must keep a financial diary to back up claims for certain deductions. Dollars and Sense reports should favorably impress any tax auditor.

Tax Records

Dollars and Sense gives you a choice of two approaches for keeping tax records. You can either set up an Account disk for recording only tax-related data, or you can record tax-related transactions as part of your regular personal Accounts, extracting the data later for tax purposes. You can also combine the two approaches, splicing tax-related Accounts into your personal Accounts set.

1. The tax disk method. Keeping tax records on a separate disk entails work and concentration, but this technique can pay off. With all tax records in one place, the balances of INCOME Accounts, withholding, itemized deduction Accounts, and so on can be transferred directly from transaction reports to tax forms. The ready-made Tax Preparation Accounts are also useful for anyone new to tax reporting. The set is so comprehensive that it resembles a flash card course in tax accounting. The Account names alone indicate which types of transactions the IRS is interested in the most.

2. Mixing tax-related transactions with regular records. Saving time is the chief advantage of this method. During the course of normal record keeping, simply identify tax-related transactions by flagging them with a `T`. You can then specify `tax-related` in transaction reports to recall the data for your tax forms.

3. A third approach. For an uncomplicated tax situation, you may decide on a compromise approach. Your basic Account set can contain Accounts intended specifically to record tax-related information. Such a set can be either a hybridized version of any ready-made set or a set you create. The Tax Preparation set will give you ideas about which tax-reporting Accounts apply to you.

Recording Transactions on the Tax Disk

To set up your tax disk, begin a new Account file with `Tax Preparation Accounts` as the initial set of Accounts (fig. 6.1).

The ready-made set contains 54 tax-related Accounts (fig. 6.2). The many income categories reflect the Internal Revenue Service's pri-

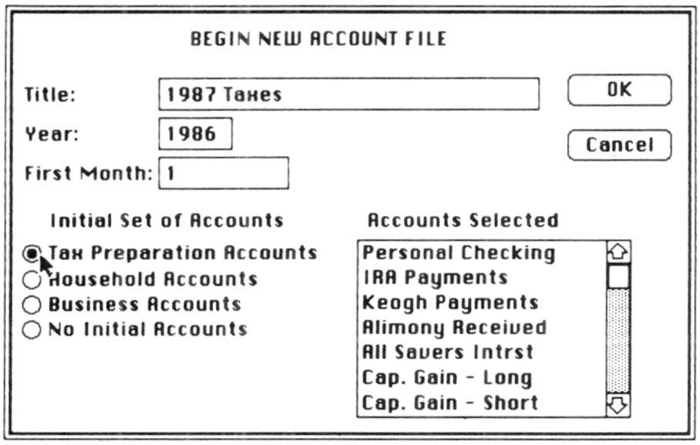

Fig. 6.1. Setting up the tax disk.

mary concern. The largest category, however, reflects your primary concern—tax-related expenses for which there may be a deduction or credit.

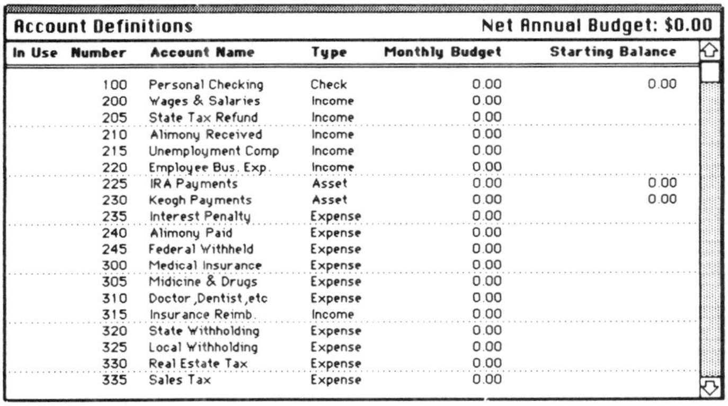

Account Definitions — **Net Annual Budget: $0.00**

In Use	Number	Account Name	Type	Monthly Budget	Starting Balance
	100	Personal Checking	Check	0.00	0.00
	200	Wages & Salaries	Income	0.00	
	205	State Tax Refund	Income	0.00	
	210	Alimony Received	Income	0.00	
	215	Unemployment Comp	Income	0.00	
	220	Employee Bus. Exp.	Income	0.00	
	225	IRA Payments	Asset	0.00	0.00
	230	Keogh Payments	Asset	0.00	0.00
	235	Interest Penalty	Expense	0.00	
	240	Alimony Paid	Expense	0.00	
	245	Federal Withheld	Expense	0.00	
	300	Medical Insurance	Expense	0.00	
	305	Midicine & Drugs	Expense	0.00	
	310	Doctor,Dentist,etc	Expense	0.00	
	315	Insurance Reimb.	Income	0.00	
	320	State Withholding	Expense	0.00	
	325	Local Withholding	Expense	0.00	
	330	Real Estate Tax	Expense	0.00	
	335	Sales Tax	Expense	0.00	

Fig. 6.2. Part of the ready-made set of Tax Preparation Accounts in the Macintosh window.

You may wonder about the numbering system for the complete set of Accounts. To establish a sense of order, the system groups categories that appear on different tax forms. INCOME Accounts, for example, jump from the 200 range to the 400 range, with ASSETS and EXPENSES sandwiched in between. EXPENSE Accounts in the 800 range are reported separately because they relate to business.

The CHECK Account

100 Personal Checking. This may be your normal checking account or one used solely for business transactions.

The INCOME Accounts

200 Wages and Salaries. Record in this Account the gross amount of all wages or salaries you receive. Be sure to create another Account if your spouse works too.

201 State Tax Refund. A state tax refund is itself taxable on the federal level for any year in which deductions were itemized in Schedule A. Refunds recorded in this Account must be reported as miscellaneous income.

202 Alimony Received. Alimony received from a former or estranged spouse must be reported as income.

203 Unemployment Compensation. Some of your unemployment compensation is taxable income. Calculate the taxable portion in this way: Add your net unemployment compensation to your adjusted gross income, then reduce the total by $12,000 if you are single or by $18,000 if you are filing a joint return. (NOTE: This formula is true for 1985. Always check current tax laws.)

303 Insurance Reimbursement. Although money received from an insurance company in settlement of a claim is non-taxable income, the amount is used to calculate casualty or theft losses.

400 Savings Interest. Interest from such sources as passbook accounts, building and loan accounts, and other savings must be reported as income. Interest under $400 appears on Schedule A or Form 1040; interest over $400 must appear on Schedule B.

401 Seller's Mortgage. If you carry any of the paper involved in the sale of a home, record as income all mortgage payments you receive.

402 Investments/Bonds. Record all net income from investments or bonds. Include any gain from the sale of property held for investment.

403 All Savers Interest. All Savers certificates allow you to earn up to $1,000 ($2,000 for married couples filing a joint return) in tax-free interest during your lifetime. Although you will not report this interest as taxable income, the amount will have an effect on any calculation of Social Security benefits.

500 Capital Gain Dividends. This amount, from mutual funds and other distributions on stock, is included in the total on line 9a of Form 1040. If the gross amount of dividends exceeds $400, you must also fill out Part II of Schedule B.

501 Taxable Dividends. Record regular dividends in this Account. These dividends will also be reported on line 9a of Form 1040. A stockholder in an American company is entitled to exclude the first $100 of dividend income every year.

502 Non-Tax Dividends. Be sure to record separately any nontaxable dividends. They can be deducted from total dividends reported.

600 Self-Employment Income. Use this Account to record your gross income if you are self-employed.

700 Capital Gains—Short. Short-term capital gains are the proceeds of the sale of a home or of such property as stocks, bonds, and cars when the properties were held for less than six months (1985 figure). This income must be reported separately from long-term gains because short-term gains are taxed at a higher rate than long-term gains.

701 Capital Gains—Long. Record capital gains on property held for longer than six months. The first 40 percent of long-term gains is tax exempt.

800 Pension/Annuity. Fully taxable pensions and annuities must be reported on lines 16, 17a, and 17b of Form 1040.

801 Rent and Royalty. You must report total rents if you own rental property. Depreciation and property expenses can be deducted as allowable expenses. The term royalties here applies to income from mineral ventures such as oil wells. Royalties from creative works such as books and plays are included in the Account you keep for gross business income.

802 Partnerships. Income from partnerships is classed as supplemental income and reported on Schedule E of Form 1040.

803 Estates and Trusts. Income from estates and trusts must be recorded. Report this income on Schedule E.

The ASSET Accounts

Your most important tax-related assets may be Individual Retirement Accounts. Each year you can invest up to $2,000 of money earned from a job. Most experts agree that IRAs or Keoghs are an essential part of any lifetime savings plan.

205 IRA Payments. Record all deposits made to your Individual Retirement Account. The amount is tax-deductible, and income from the account is tax-deferred during your entire working life.

206 Keogh Payments. Keogh plans are IRAs for the self-employed, whether full- or part-time. You can contribute up to 20 percent of self-employed income to a maximum contribution of $30,000 a year.

The EXPENSE Accounts

All deductions, itemized or not, that you claim must be distributed accurately. Keep all receipts, sales slips, and other documentation to back your claim in the event of an audit. These are the essential EXPENSE Accounts:

235 Interest Penalty. Any interest penalty you pay as a result of early withdrawal of savings may be used to adjust your income (Form 1040, item 27).

240 Alimony Paid. Any legally required alimony that you pay is used to adjust your income (Form 1040, item 28).

245 Federal Tax Withheld. You must report all withholding. You find this information on your paycheck stub. At the end of the year, check the totals against your W-2 forms. This Account can also be used to record estimated tax paid, but separate Accounts are more convenient to use.

300 Medical Insurance. Under most circumstances, money you spend on medical insurance can be included in the medical expense itemized deduction (Schedule A, item 4a). In 1985, total medical expenses must exceed five percent of your adjusted gross income to be claimed.

305 Medicine and Drugs. Medicine and drugs are allowed as itemized deductions (Schedule A, item 1).

310 Doctor and Dentist. Record all payments to doctors and dentists and report them on line 4a of Schedule A.

311 State Withholding. Keep a record of any state withholding. State taxes withheld are listed as an itemized deduction at line 8 of Schedule A.

325 Local Withholding. Local taxes withheld are also reported on line 8 of Schedule A. State and local taxes on motor fuels used in a business can also be deducted.

330 Real Estate Tax. Real estate taxes are deductible on Schedule A.

335 Sales Tax. At the end of the year, use your state tax table to calculate sales tax on the many small items you buy. This Account can be used to record extraordinary payments such as an outright purchase of a car.

340 Auto Registration. Your registration fee can be part of your use of automobile deduction.

345 Mortgage Interest. Your largest interest deduction may be your mortgage. When you record mortgage payments, always distribute the interest to this Account. Report personal interest expenses on line 13 of Schedule A.

Record interest on business loans in a separate Account, and report this interest on Schedule C or E.

350 Credit Card Interest. Interest paid on credit or charge cards is deductible (line 14 of Schedule A).

355 Loan Interest. Record interest paid on other personal loans in this Account.

360 Cash Contributions. You can deduct contributions to certain charities, including churches and relief organizations. In 1985 the maximum deduction for contributions (cash and non-cash combined) is 50 percent of your adjusted gross income.

365 Non-Cash Contributions. Record the value of such non-cash contributions as clothing, food, and works of art. When the value of an item exceeds $200, keep particularly careful records to whom the contribution was given, where you got the contribution, and its fair market value.

370 Casualty Losses. Major losses from catastrophes such as fire, flooding, earthquake, or theft are deductible. In 1985 the law is that a loss is deductible to the extent that the loss exceeds 10 percent of your adjusted gross income. Casualty losses are reported on Schedule A and detailed on Form 4684.

375 Union Dues. Union dues are classed as miscellaneous deductions at line 22 of Schedule A.

380 Educational Expenses. Educational expenses are deductible if the expenses are for improving skills related to your current work or are required by law or by an employer as a condition for keeping your job.

385 Accountant. The services of an accountant to prepare your taxes are deductible. You can also use this Account to record books or computer programs, such as Dollars and Sense, that you buy to help prepare your taxes, as well as the price of admission to all seminars and lectures about tax preparation.

390 Miscellaneous. Use this Account for those tax-related expenses not covered elsewhere. Such expenses as the cost of moving or finding a new job probably are not frequent enough in your life to merit separate Accounts.

820 Advertising. In estimating business profit or loss, advertising is an allowable deduction, listed on item 6 of Schedule C.

825 Automobile. Record actual expenses for a car used solely for business. Include depreciation, oil, and gas. As an alternative, create a Mileage Account and calculate your mileage allowance monthly. You can use both Accounts and decide at the end of the year which method will bring the larger deduction.

830 Depreciation. You can claim depreciation on certain business property including buildings, machinery, vehicles, and computers.

835 Insurance. Insurance payments connected with your business are deductible.

840 Interest. Record interest paid on all business loans.

845 Legal and Accounting. Record those fees paid to lawyers and accountants that apply to running your business. Do not include any legal or accounting expenses incurred in preparing your personal income taxes.

855 Rent Paid. Keep a record of all rent paid to maintain an office or factory. This is reported as a business deduction.

860 Repairs/Maintenance. You are entitled to deduct all repair and maintenance costs of any rental property you own.

865 Telephone/Utility. Keep a record of all telephone and utility bills that are business-related.

870 Travel/Entertainment. Travel and entertainment costs that are related to business must be reported on Schedule C, Profit Loss from Business or Profession.

875 Wages. This Account records wages paid to your employees.

998 Check Charges. This is the mandatory Account for recording check charges. You can change the name and number, but the Check Charges Account cannot be deleted from the set.

Additional Accounts

The ready-made set of Tax Preparation Accounts is comprehensive enough for most tax reporting. Like the household set, however, you may need additional Accounts to suit your financial picture. You may want to add the following Accounts to your set:

INCOME Accounts: Commissions, Dismissal Pay, Fees, Gifts, Overtime Pay, Pensions, Premiums, Prizes, Social Security Benefits, Tips, Unemployment Benefits.

EXPENSE Accounts: Child Care, Clothing for Business, Equipment and Machinery, Estimated Tax, FICA, Home Office Rent, Mileage, Supplies.

The Tax Flag

If you decide to incorporate all tax-related transactions into your personal or regular business records, you need to identify those transactions as tax-related. One way to accomplish this identification is to keep certain Accounts for tax-related transactions only.

Keeping separate Accounts for the two types of transactions, however, can result in an unmanageable list, in which case you can store all transactions together. Tax-related transactions are easily extracted as long as the transactions are properly flagged with T in the entry screen. For example, if you claim business entertainment as an itemized deduction, you can call for a transaction report of only the T-flagged transactions in the Entertainment Account.

Editing: Personal Checking — Balance: $ 1,348.00

Clear	Check	Date	Description	Dist. Account	Tax	Check($)	Deposit($)
-	5005	08/10	Lunch with Schmidt	Entertainment	T	45.00	
-	5006	08/10	Dinner with Mom	Entertainment	-	30.00	

Fig. 6.3. A transaction report can recover T*-flagged transactions from any Account.*

Reporting Income and Expenses

In only a second or two, Dollars and Sense can report your total income and expenses for the tax year. Choose Income Statement from the Report Menu, and specify Annual (fig. 6.4). Statements of income and expenses appear. You can easily pick out the proper figures for your tax forms.

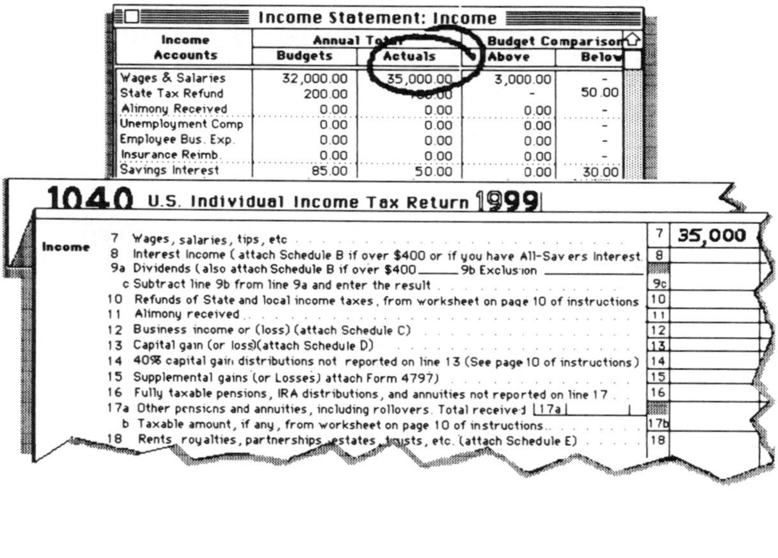

Fig. 6.4. A year's income recalled in an income statement.

Calculate gross income first. For tax purposes, gross income includes wages, salaries, tips, interest, dividends, rents, royalties, retirement plans, estate and trust income, and the proceeds of partnerships or proprietorships. Calculate and report separately such other income categories as interest, capital gains and losses, and dividends because those incomes are taxed under different rules. You can then find your adjusted gross income by reducing your total income by such allowable adjustments as moving expenses, alimony payments, depreciation, amortization, and depletion.

The second part of the Income Statement shows expenses for the year (fig. 6.5). If you use the recommended tax-related Accounts, you will have no trouble transferring many of these figures to your tax forms.

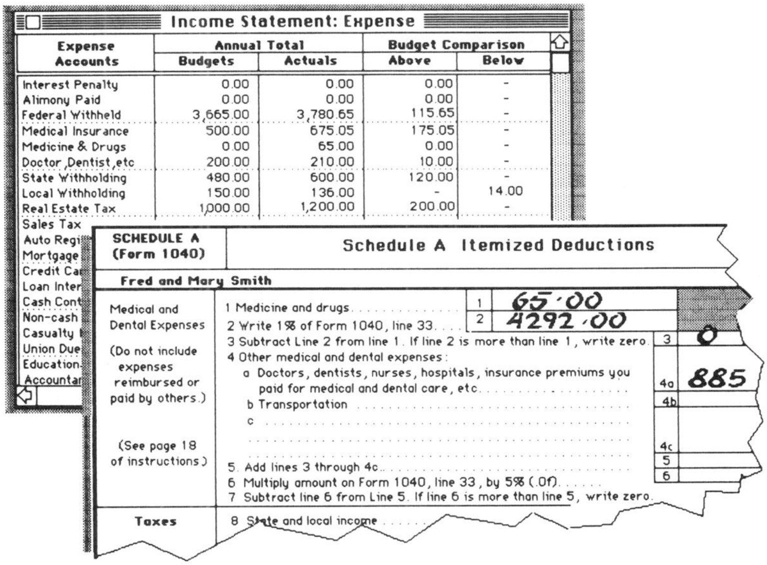

Income Statement: Expense

Expense Accounts	Annual Total		Budget Comparison	
	Budgets	Actuals	Above	Below
Interest Penalty	0.00	0.00	0.00	-
Alimony Paid	0.00	0.00	0.00	-
Federal Withheld	3,665.00	3,780.65	115.65	-
Medical Insurance	500.00	675.05	175.05	-
Medicine & Drugs	0.00	65.00	0.00	-
Doctor,Dentist,etc	200.00	210.00	10.00	-
State Withholding	480.00	600.00	120.00	-
Local Withholding	150.00	136.00	-	14.00
Real Estate Tax	1,000.00	1,200.00	200.00	-
Sales Tax				
Auto Regi				
Mortgage				
Credit Ca				
Loan Inter				
Cash Cont				
Non-cash				
Casualty				
Union Due				
Education				
Accountar				

SCHEDULE A (Form 1040) — Schedule A Itemized Deductions

Fred and Mary Smith

Medical and Dental Expenses (Do not include expenses reimbursed or paid by others.) (See page 18 of instructions.)

1 Medicine and drugs . . . 1 65·00
2 Write 1% of Form 1040, line 33 . . . 2 4292·00
3 Subtract Line 2 from line 1. If line 2 is more than line 1, write zero. 3 0
4 Other medical and dental expenses:
a Doctors, dentists, nurses, hospitals, insurance premiums you paid for medical and dental care, etc. . . . 4a 885
b Transportation . . . 4b
c . . . 4c
5 Add lines 3 through 4c . . . 5
6 Multiply amount on Form 1040, line 33, by 5% (.05) . . . 6
7 Subtract line 6 from Line 5. If line 6 is more than line 5, write zero.

Taxes — 8 State and local income . . .

Fig. 6.5. A year's expenses recalled in the second part of the Income Statement.

You can easily extract tax-related transactions that are part of your regular records. For every Account that may contain tax-related transactions, call for a transaction report for the complete year, specifying `Tax Item` only. The report details only those transactions flagged with T. The summary gives a total, not of the balance of the Account, but of tax-related transactions only (fig. 6.6).

Transaction Summary

T x	Date Mo/Da/Yr	Transaction Title	Distribution Account	Amounts ($) Decrease	Amounts ($) Increase
T	06/01/84	Lunch with Fiori	American Express		55.00
T	06/05/84	Worldco lunch	American Express		86.77
T	06/18/84	Dinner with Gunn	American Express		102.99
T	08/08/84	Lunch with Schmidt	Personal Checking		45.00
T	08/30/84	Dinner with 3D Graphics	Personal Checking		65.50
T	09/02/84	Dinner with 3D Graphics	Personal Checking		89.00
T	09/11/84	Reception for Schmidt Inc	Personal Checking		356.75

Account YTD Summary

Accounts Num	Accounts Name	Accounts Type	Number Tran..	Total Amount	Current Balance
100	Personal Checking	Check	4	(556.25)	(344.25)
303	American Express	Liability	3	([illegible])	(2,276.04)
530	Entertainment	Expense	7	801.01	801.01

Fig. 6.6. Tax-deductible expenses extracted from the Entertainment Account.

Planning for Estimated Taxes

Those who estimate taxes must make saving for estimated taxes a high priority because you can be penalized heavily for not paying them on time. Use Dollars and Sense to earmark and keep track of contingency savings (see Chapter 5).

Keep money put aside for estimated taxes in either a regular passbook savings account or a money market account. If the account includes check-writing services, enter the account as a CHECK Account, otherwise make the account an ASSET Account (fig. 6.7). Be sure also to set up Dollars and Sense Accounts to record the payments you make. You need two EXPENSE Accounts: an Estimated Federal Account and an Estimated State Account. You can assign budgets to the accounts for the amount you need to save each month, or variable budgets showing exactly when the payments are due.

Account Definitions

In Use	Number	Account Name	Type	Monthly Budget	Starting Balance
	170	Savings	Asset	600.00	
	611	Estimated Federal	Expense	300.00	
	612	Estimated State	Expense	40.00	

Fig. 6.7. New Estimated-Tax Accounts.

Federal and state estimated taxes are due in April, June, September, and January. For the sake of illustration, suppose you have just paid the first installment in April and are contemplating the June installment. You have two months to save $600 for federal taxes plus $80 for state taxes. Every two weeks you can transfer $170 from your checking to your savings account, either electronically or by check. Although you write only one check, make your Savings Account the Base Account and record the money as two apparent deposits (fig. 6.8).

Fig. 6.8. Deposit for estimated taxes.

Entering: Savings

Base Account	Date	Description	Dist. Account	Tax	Decrease	Increase
Savings	04/21	Estimated State	Personal Checking	T		20.00
Savings	04/21	Estimated Federal	Personal Checking	T		150.00

Your savings are increased by the total amount, but by separating the payment into two sums with different description fields, you simplify keeping track of how much you have saved toward each goal. ***Be sure you write descriptions exactly the same way each time. If you fail to do so, transactions can be missed when a report is called for.***

Figure 6.9 shows the effect of the savings deposits on their source, Personal Checking. This method reduces the CHECK Account by the correct $170, but records the single check as two "miscellaneous" checks.

Fig. 6.9. Effect of transactions on the Personal Checking Account.

Editing: Personal Checking

Clear	Check	Date	Description	Dist. Account	Tax	Check($)	Deposit($)
-	Misc	04/21	Estimated State Tax	Savings Account	T	20.00	
-	Misc	04/21	Estimated Federal Tax	Savings Account	T	150.00	

You can also save time by creating an automatic set for the transfer. This set can be reactivated regularly, either weekly, biweekly, or monthly. Alternatively, you can ignore scheduling and simply transfer lump sums at your convenience. The important principle is that you record separately savings for different goals. In this way, you can set priorities and track progress toward those goals.

Keeping Track of Estimated Taxes

At any time before a bill is due, you can see if you have saved enough to pay the bill. To do this, call for a transaction report of the Savings Account and specify the savings goal in the `Title` field (fig. 6.10). For example, to see how close to your estimated federal tax payment you are, you can type *Estimated Federal* or *Federal*. In fact, you can type just *Feder*, and Dollars and Sense will do the rest. Bear in mind, however, that Dollars and Sense will search for anything with *Feder* in it, so anything with the word *Federal* (Federal Savings and Loan, Federal Express, etc.) will be recalled. You may wish to code the savings fund in a unique way to avoid the possibility of calling up the wrong Account.

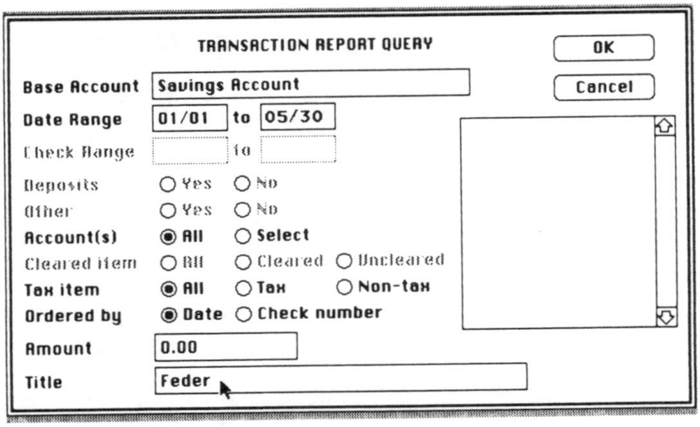

Fig. 6.10. The transaction query box.

The transaction report appears in two parts (fig. 6.11). Individual amounts with dates of deposit are shown first; the follow-up summary shows the total saved for estimated federal tax and also the balance of the Savings Account.

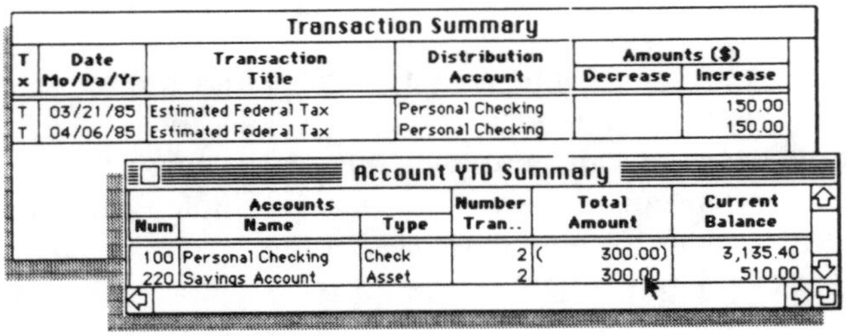
Transaction Summary
T x
Date Mo/Da/Yr
Transaction Title
Distribution Account
Amounts ($)
Decrease
Increase
T 03/21/85 Estimated Federal Tax Personal Checking 150.00
T 04/06/85 Estimated Federal Tax Personal Checking 150.00
Account YTD Summary
Accounts
Num
Name
Type
Number Tran..
Total Amount
Current Balance
100 Personal Checking Check 2 (300.00) 3,135.40
220 Savings Account Asset 2 300.00 510.00

Fig. 6.11. The transaction report of amounts saved for estimated taxes.

This report is probably most interesting shortly before taxes are due. You will have not only adequate warning of your capacity to pay, but also time to work out alternative strategies if necessary.

Paying Estimated Taxes

If your Savings Account is a CHECK Account, you can pay the IRS directly. Record the payment with Savings as the Base Account (see fig. 6.12).

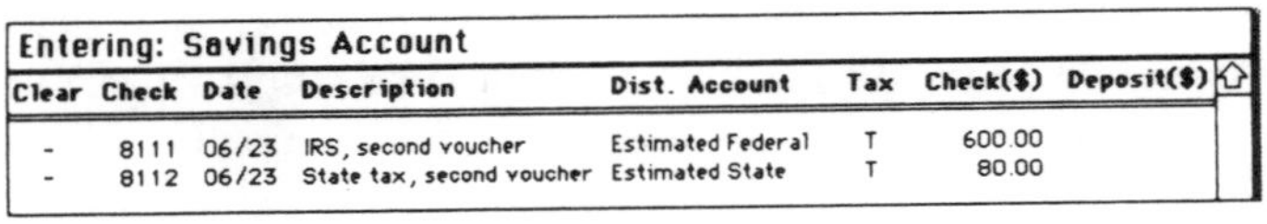
Entering: Savings Account
Clear Check Date Description Dist. Account Tax Check($) Deposit($)
- 8111 06/23 IRS, second voucher Estimated Federal T 600.00
- 8112 06/23 State tax, second voucher Estimated State T 80.00

Fig. 6.12. Payment of estimated tax from a CHECK Account.

This time you can make a true Account distribution. Your Savings Account balance is decreased by the payment while the amount you paid is recorded in an Estimated Tax Account.

If your Savings Account is an ASSET Account, transfer the amount of the payment to the CHECK Account that will actually pay the tax (fig. 6.13). Record an electronic transfer as `Misc`; otherwise the transaction should be recorded as a `deposit`. Write the check to the IRS as you normally would.

Fig. 6.13. Payment of estimated tax from an ASSET Account.

Entering: Personal Checking

Clear	Check	Date	Description	Dist. Account	Tax	Check($)	Deposit($)
-	Misc	06/22	Transfer for Est. Federal	Savings Account	-		600.00
-	8020	06/23	IRS, second voucher	Estimated Federal	T	600.00	

7
Business Applications for Dollars and Sense

Now that you are beginning to feel comfortable with the Dollars and Sense program, you are ready to try some business applications. This chapter will show how Dollars and Sense can help you accomplish the common money management tasks essential for a smoothly run business. Look for ideas and examples that you will be able to adapt to your own situation. To get the most out of the following pages, you need at least a working knowledge of Dollars and Sense techniques, all of which are covered in earlier sections of this book and in the manual that came with your program.

Bookkeeping in General

As a record keeping and reporting program, Dollars and Sense can help control the financial development and running of your business. The program has all the capabilities of a classic bookkeeping system: the efficient recording, classifying, and summarizing of financial business information. You can safely store records of all your business transactions in Dollars and Sense files with the confidence that the data can be recalled easily when needed.

Dollars and Sense and traditional bookkeeping techniques do have several important characteristics in common:

1. Dollars and Sense provides a way of keeping a systematic record of daily business activity using double-entry bookkeeping.

2. The program classifies transactions into related categories (Accounts).

3. Dollars and Sense summarizes financial information in reports and graphs. The summaries can help control money and suggest fiscal strategies as well as provide the data needed for reporting to regulatory agencies.

The real aim of Dollars and Sense and double-entry bookkeeping is to balance the accounting equation: Assets = Liabilities + Owner's Equity (net worth). Something is wrong if both sides are not equal, because each side represents the same business resources. The left side of the equation represents what resources are owned by the business; the right side shows where the resources came from.

The Business Accounts

Dollars and Sense gives you a ready-made set of 59 Accounts applicable to almost any business (fig. 7.1). When you start your first Dollars and Sense business file, transfer the ready-made set to your file, rather than creating your own from scratch. You can easily delete unnecessary Accounts and add new Accounts peculiar to your own business.

Account Definitions — **Net Annual Budget: $0.00**

In Use	Number	Account Name	Type	Monthly Budget	Starting Balance
	100	Checking Account	Check	0.00	0.00
	200	Acc'ts Receivable	Asset	0.00	0.00
	205	Accum Depreciation	Asset	0.00	0.00
	210	Allowance/Bad Debt	Asset	0.00	0.00
	215	Buildings	Asset	0.00	0.00
	220	Cash on Hand	Asset	0.00	0.00
	225	Furniture/Fixtures	Asset	0.00	0.00
	230	Goodwill	Asset	0.00	0.00
	235	Inventory	Asset	0.00	0.00
	240	Investments	Asset	0.00	0.00
	245	Land	Asset	0.00	0.00
	250	Machines/Equipment	Asset	0.00	0.00
	255	Prepaid Items	Asset	0.00	0.00
	260	Vehicles	Asset	0.00	0.00
	300	Acc'ts Payable	Liability	0.00	0.00
	305	Mortgage/Lease	Liability	0.00	0.00
	310	Notes Payable	Liability	0.00	0.00
	315	Taxes Payable	Liability	0.00	0.00
×	400	Check Interest	Income	0.00	

Fig. 7.1. The Business Accounts on the Macintosh screen.

Making Business Decisions with the Account Definitions Window

The account definitions window can operate as a spreadsheet to help you isolate problems and test solutions. The net annual budget balance tells you how your projected expenses compare with your predicted income. A positive figure shows your likely profit, but a negative amount indicates a net loss.

Your Dollars and Sense program can produce reports to let you know how proposed changes can affect your business. If you are considering acquiring a new plant or machinery, or hiring or firing employees, set up a Dollars and Sense business file with new budgets. For minor changes use your current file; however, set up a new file for extensive or complex changes. Make sure you have Accounts for every element of your proposal such as Sales, Salaries, Inventory, and so on.

Here is is a common profitability problem that can be solved by using the Account definitions screen:

Problem: You are trying to decide whether to hire a new salesperson. You feel sure this salesperson can increase sales by 20 percent, but you need to know how much you can afford to pay.

Solution: First increase the gross sales budget by 20 percent, then set budgets for all the Accounts affected by the hiring, such as the Salary, Withholding, Expenses, Utilities, and Cost of Goods Accounts. The net annual budget balance shows the increase in income offset by the cost of the new employee. If this is not an acceptable profit, with allowance for error and the unforeseen, you can change your Salary Account budget (and withholding) to see what you can offer a new employee.

Owner's Equity and the Balance Sheet

The owner's equity is the owner's resources invested in a business. Equity can show the owner's net worth, calculated by subtracting liabilities from assets. The owner's equity includes both the initial investment and earnings from the profitable operation of the business.

A healthy enterprise's equity increases as business grows, and decreases if the company is unprofitable or if the owner withdraws cash or other assets. Dollars and Sense can help you keep track of fluctuations in equity by supplying reports showing the specific areas gaining or losing equity.

Figure 7.2 shows an example of the Accounts and starting balances for a new photographic business housed rent-free in the owner's home.

Account Definitions

In Use	Number	Account Name	Type	Monthly Budget	Starting Balance
x	998	Check Charges	Expense	0.00	
x	999	Check Interest	Income	0.00	
	100	Business Checking	Check	0.00	5,500.00
	200	Truck	Asset	0.00	7,000.00
	201	Cameras	Asset	0.00	2,000.00
	202	Furniture/Fittings	Asset	0.00	6,000.00
	203	Inventory	Asset	0.00	2,000.00
	300	Truck loan	Liability	0.00	5,000.00
	301	Furniture Loan	Liability	0.00	6,000.00

Fig. 7.2. Some Accounts and starting balances for a new business.

The balance sheet report shows that the photographer's equity is $11,500 (fig. 7.3). This figure represents his own money in cash, assets, and down payments. In addition to his own equity, he has taken out loans for the truck and furniture totaling $11,000.

Analysis of Balance Sheet: Asset

Asset Accounts	Distribution (%)		Totals for Year		Act as % of Bdgt
	Budgets	Actuals	Budgets	Actuals	
Business Checking	24.44	24.44	5,500.00	5,500.00	100.00
Truck	31.11	31.11	7,000.00	7,000.00	100.00
Cameras	8.89	8.89	2,000.00	2,000.00	100.00
Furniture/Fittings	26.67	26.67	6,000.00	6,000.00	100.00
Inventory	8.89	8.89	2,000.00	2,000.00	100.00
[Totals]	100.00	100.00	22,500.00	22,500.00	100.00

Analysis of Balance Sheet: Liability

Liability Accounts	Distribution (%)		Totals for Year		Act as % of Bdgt
	Budgets	Actuals	Budgets	Actuals	
Truck loan	22.22	22.22	5,000.00	5,000.00	100.00
Furniture Loan	26.67	26.67	6,000.00	6,000.00	100.00
[Totals]	48.89	48.89	11,000.00	11,000.00	100.00
[Net]	51.11	51.11	11,500.00	11,500.00	100.00

Fig. 7.3. The balance sheet analysis showing net worth for a new company.

The balance sheet shows your financial position on a particular date. Your financial picture is constantly evolving, and the balance sheet is a way of showing just how you stand. All businesses prepare balance sheets at the end of the year, but most balance sheets are updated monthly or quarterly.

Entering Transactions with the Drawing Account

Some businessmen put themselves on their own payroll and record the money they retain in a Salary Account. Others draw cash or pay their personal bills directly from the company bank account. Drawing cash for personal use must always be recorded, because such withdrawals decrease the owner's equity. Handle such withdrawals by creating an ASSET Account called Drawing (fig. 7.4).

File Edit Select

Account Definitions

In Use	Number	Account Name	Type	Monthly Budget	Starting Balance
	204	Drawing Account	Asset	0.00	0.00

Fig. 7.4. Creating the Drawing Account.

Whenever you withdraw cash or pay your personal bills out of company funds, you take the amount from your Drawing Account. Actually, you should reduce this Account with the value of any of the merchandise you take for yourself and any barter items. The Drawing Account, which is really a way of getting money out of your business, will reduce the business's net worth and the liability the business owes the owner (owner's equity).

Record the $500 you withdraw from the company bank account at the end of the month in the Business Checking Account as shown in figure 7.5.

Entering: Business Checking

Clear	Check	Date	Description	Dist. Account	Tax	Check($)	Deposit($)
-	4055	05/01	Personal Cash	Drawing Account	-	500.00	

Fig. 7.5. Using the Drawing Account.

Entering Direct Payment Transactions

The owner or bookkeeper of a small business can use Dollars and Sense for recording daily transactions such as sales and purchases whether by credit or cash. How you record your transactions will depend on your own needs. A bookstore owner may not want to record every used paperback sold for 25 cents, but a lawyer will want an accurate list of each phone call made on behalf of clients.

The following examples of transaction entry can be used as models or adapted to your business needs. They are arranged in order of increasing complexity. Almost all the Accounts used are in the ready-made business set. The exception is the addition of an INCOME Account called Gross Receipts, which provides both a record of income and a means of balancing Account distributions.

Service Calls

Most businesses can be divided into two categories—those that offer services and those that sell goods. Some businesses, however, fall somewhere in between, such as plumbers or electrical repair specialists who sell retail items from a store as well as make service calls.

Using the plumber as an example, look at the many different transactions the average independent businessman may encounter. A plumber's simplest transaction can be the home service call to tighten a washer or readjust a valve. If the customer pays by check, the plumber can go back to the shop and record the payment in his Dollars and Sense Business Checking Account (fig. 7.6).

Entering: Business Checking

Clear	Check	Date	Description	Dist. Account	Tax	Check($)	Deposit($)
-	Deposit	01/03	Job #234 Serv. call	Gross Receipts	T		125.00

Fig. 7.6. A check distributed to the Gross Receipts Account.

The payment transaction is recorded in two Accounts, the deposit entered in Business Checking and a record of the payment in Gross Receipts. Distribution increases the balance of Gross Receipts because the Gross Receipts Account is an INCOME Account.

If a service call includes replacing a flow meter, for example, the plumber must account for the component's cost and record the effect on the parts inventory with a multiple distribution (fig. 7.7).

Entering: Business Checking

Clear	Check	Date	Description	Dist. Account	Tax	Check($)	Deposit($)
-	Deposit	05/15	Job # 753, Serv, call	-Multiple-	T		150.00
				Gross Receipts	T	150.00	
				Inventory	T		15.00
				Cost of Goods Sold	T	15.00	

Fig. 7.7. A multiple distribution.

The plumber can make a multiple distribution of the transaction by shifting the amount of the check, the cost for the flow meter, and the reduction of parts inventory between columns. Both the credit and debit sides of the equation balance. The $15 amount charged for parts is deducted from the Inventory ASSET Account, while the same amount is added to the Cost of Goods Sold, an EXPENSE Account.

Inventory Purchases

At some point, the plumber needs to replenish inventory. A purchase of 20 flow meters is recorded in the CHECK Account, and at the same time the Inventory ASSET Account is updated. Any freight charge must also be recorded (fig. 7.8).

Entering: Business Checking

Clear	Check	Date	Description	Dist. Account	Tax	Check($)	Deposit($)
-	2001	07/15	20 Acme 200's @ $3.50	-Multiple-	T	80.00	
				Inventory	T		70.00
				Freight	T		10.00

Fig. 7.8. Freight charges must be included when inventory is replenished.

Retail Sales and Sales Tax

Your sales transactions can be recorded easily in Dollars and Sense in a variety of ways. Before entering your first sale, decide how you will record any sales taxes levied by your state and local government. You may decide to record sales without regard for taxes; then at the end of each accounting period, calculate the tax as a percentage of total sales (fig. 7.9).

Entering: Business Checking

Clear	Check	Date	Description	Dist. Account	Tax	Check($)	Deposit($)
-	Deposit	07/16	A1 Garbage King unit	-Multiple-	T		95.00
				Sales	T	95.00	
				Inventory	T	40.00	
				Cost of Goods Sold	T		40.00

Fig. 7.9. Sales tax may be calculated later.

Using this method of showing the tax collected, recall the total sales with a transaction report and calculate the tax due at the end of the accounting period. Your tax payment is distributed to Taxes, an EXPENSE Account. When you send a check to the appropriate tax authority, record the transaction as shown in figure 7.10.

Entering: Business Checking

Clear	Check	Date	Description	Dist. Account	Tax	Check($)	Deposit($)
-	2002	07/16	Sales Tax for June	Taxes	-	2,000.00	

Fig. 7.10. The sales tax payment distribution.

An alternative method helps you keep the most accurate tax records by showing the breakdown of price and tax on each transaction as you enter the figures. The extra time involved keeps records of taxable items completely separate from nontaxable purchases. The second plan of handling sales tax is suited for businesses involved in taxable and nontaxable transactions. Look at figure 7.11 for the way to record this transaction.

Entering: Business Checking

Clear	Check	Date	Description	Dist. Account	Tax	Check($)	Deposit($)
-	Deposit	07/16	A1 Garbage King unit	-Multiple-	T		95.00
				Sales	T	87.00	
				Taxes Payable	T	8.00	
				Inventory	T	40.00	
				Cost of Goods Sold	T		40.00

Fig. 7.11. In this example, the sales tax is recorded with the transaction.

In this way the sales tax is deducted at the point of the original transaction and recorded as a LIABILITY. One of the advantages of this method is you have a clear picture of the net worth of your business. Sales tax becomes a liability that must be paid. Recording the payment is almost the same with both methods, but in this situation the payment is distributed to the Taxes Payable Account.

Credit Card Sales

Payments by bank credit cards, such as VISA or MasterCard, are treated like ordinary checks in Dollars and Sense (fig. 7.12). The payments are instantly redeemable and can be deposited directly into your business bank account. The payment is entered as miscellaneous under the Check column, and the amount must be shifted to show the payment as a deposit. Remember to record your bank card's monthly service and handling charge in a Check Charges Account at the end of the month.

Entering: Business Checking

Clear	Check	Date	Description	Dist. Account	Tax	Check($)	Deposit($)
-	Misc	07/29	Washers, VISA	-Multiple-	T		25.00
				Sales	T	23.50	
				Taxes Payable	-	1.50	
				Inventory	T	10.00	
				Cost of Goods Sold	T		10.00

Fig. 7.12. Credit card payments are treated like check payments.

You can determine your percentage of credit card sales with transaction reports. You can further refine your question by specifying the name of the bank card in the title field of the report query.

Hard Cash Transactions

The movement of hard cash through a business is difficult to track accurately. Dollars and Sense offers you better control over hard cash transactions.

Some businesses handle so many cash sales that recording them all in Dollars and Sense becomes impractical. A store that sells used books, for example, may make hundreds of weekly transactions, many of them involving individually small amounts of hard cash. In such cases, the time to use Dollars and Sense is at the end of the week or whenever the contents of the cash register are deposited in the bank. The cash deposit record could look like the example shown in figure 7.13.

Editing: Business Checking

Clear	Check	Date	Description	Dist. Account	Tax	Check($)	Deposit($)
-	Deposit	07/21	Cash receipts	-Multiple-	-		1,500.00
				Sales	T	1,425.00	
				Taxes Payable	T	75.00	

Fig. 7.13. A weekly cash deposit for a store.

As you record your hard cash transactions, you can decide whether your business requires that you maintain an Account for your reduction in inventory. If you are selling used paperback books, you may be satisfied with an educated guess about the number of books you have on hand. If you, however, are selling first editions and collectibles, you will watch your inventory closely.

You can also set up a Cash on Hand Account to keep track of the money you carry for cash business purchases during the day. Owners of stores that sell used books normally keep a supply of cash to pay for books brought to the store. Look at figure 7.14 to see how your Dollars and Sense transaction would record the amount actually deposited in the bank, the total amount of sales, the taxes payable, and the increase in cash on hand.

Editing: Business Checking

Clear	Check	Date	Description	Dist. Account	Tax	Check($)	Deposit($)
-	Deposit	07/21	Cash receipts	-Multiple-	-		860.00
				Sales	T	1,000.00	
				Cash on Hand	T		200.00
				Taxes Payable	T	60.00	

Fig. 7.14. Using a Cash on Hand Account for business cash purchases.

When the bookstore owner purchases a used book for cash, the transaction is entered with Cash on Hand as the Base Account. In this case, distribute purchases to the Inventory Account (fig. 7.15).

Entering: Cash on Hand

Base Account	Date	Description	Dist. Account	Tax	Decrease	Increase
Cash on Hand	07/30	Proust, 1st edition	Inventory	T	40.00	

Fig. 7.15. Recording a cash purchase.

Accounts Receivable and Accounts Payable

Although designed for cash-based businesses, Dollars and Sense can be an efficient system for recording and tracking accounts receivable and payable. The size of your business will determine how you maintain these transactions. If you have few transactions for accounts receivable and payable, you can keep them in Accounts on your regular disk. If you have many accounts receivable and accounts payable, you should keep them on a separate file.

Accounts Receivable

Use the single Accounts Receivable ASSET Account as the Base Account for recording accounts receivable transactions. You can keep track of uncollected amounts with later transaction reports that can be used as invoices. When the account is paid, amounts are deposited directly into the Business Checking Account and distributed to the Accounts Receivable Account.

A simple example of an Accounts Receivable transaction is when the plumber leaves a bill for a service call and parts (fig. 7.16).

Entering: Acc'ts Receivable

Base Account	Date	Description	Dist. Account	Tax	Decrease	Increase
Acc'ts Receivable	01/07	Job #1345 Serv. Call	-Multiple-	T		150.00
			Gross Receipts	T	150.00	
			Cost of Goods Sold	T		15.00
			Inventory	T	15.00	

Fig. 7.16. Recording an accounts receivable transaction.

To make this distribution work properly, add a distribution line after Gross Receipts. New distribution lines can be added by using `Insert Dist. Line` from the Edit Menu. You also need to shift the last amount to the correct column. Click the `Switch Column` button or press the S key to relocate the amount. In this way, you have increased the Accounts Receivable, Gross Receipts, and Cost of Goods Accounts, while reducing the Inventory Account.

The plumber has entered in the description field a job number that will probably link to a separate "job book" that lists the name and address of the customer, details of the parts used, and so on. By indicating that a transaction report should follow the entry, the plumber can instantly produce the data he needs for a bill. The plumber can even use the report itself as an invoice (fig. 7.17).

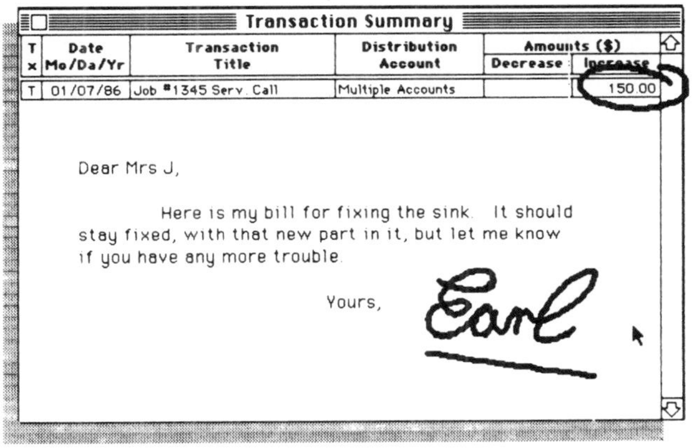

Fig. 7.17. Using a transaction summary as a bill.

A transaction paid partly in cash with the balance due at a later date is recorded in a different way. Accounts Receivable is again the Base Account (fig. 7.18).

Entering: Acc'ts Receivable

Base Account	Date	Description	Dist. Account	Tax	Decrease	Increase
Acc'ts Receivable	02/03	Job #280, Service & pa...	-Multiple-	T		100.00
			Business Checking	T		50.00
			Gross Receipts	T	150.00	
			Cost of Goods Sold	T		15.00
			Inventory	T	15.00	

Fig. 7.18. Recording a partial payment in an Accounts Receivable Account.

You will need to insert a distribution line and shift the last amount for this transaction to be entered properly.

When the customer does pay, you can record the transaction in the Business Checking Account (fig. 7.19) or in any other CHECK Account you designate to receive the deposit. Your deposit reduces Accounts Receivable by the amount of the customer's payment. To avoid rebilling, recall your original entry in Accounts Receivable and edit your description field to record "paid."

Entering: Business Checking

Clear	Check	Date	Description	Dist. Account	Tax	Check($)	Deposit($)
-	Deposit	08/01	#1345, Mrs J. Chk#12...	Acc'ts Receivable	T		150.00

Fig. 7.19. Entering the balance of the payment in business checking.

Accounts Payable

If you keep your records on one disk, record liabilities that result from buying supplies or merchandise on credit in the LIABILITY Account called Accounts Payable (fig. 7.20). When you pay, enter the check in the Business Checking Account with the distribution to Accounts Payable (fig. 7.21).

Entering: Acc'ts Payable

Base Account	Date	Description	Dist. Account	Tax	Purchase	Payment
Acc'ts Payable	06/26	RotoBot pump #8901	-Multiple-	T	450.00	
			Inventory	T		425.00
			Freight	T		25.00

Fig. 7.20. Credit purchases go on an Accounts Payable LIABILITY Account.

Entering: Business Checking

Clear	Check	Date	Description	Dist. Account	Tax	Check($)	Deposit($)
-	3004	07/21	RotoRobo Pumps Inc.	Acc'ts Payable	T	450.00	

Fig. 7.21. Recording a payment to the Accounts Payable Account.

Just as Accounts Receivable handled partial payments, transaction reports can be used to keep track of the amount you still owe on the Accounts Payable Account and produce a payment schedule (fig. 7.22). A transaction summary shows that Accounts Payable has been appropriately reduced by the payment. When your payment clears the amount due, your balance is zero.

Transaction Summary

T x	Date Mo/Da/Yr	Transaction Title	Distribution Account	Amounts ($) Payment	Purchase
T	06/26/86	RotoBot pump #8901	Multiple Accounts		450.00
T	07/21/86	RotoRobo Pumps Inc.	Business Checking	450.00	

Fig. 7.22. A transaction summary keeps track of the Accounts Payable Account.

Aging Accounts Receivable and Payable

As you have seen, transaction reports are used to "age" outstanding receivables and payables. The simplest method is to call for a transaction report with a date range—possibly 10, 20 or 30 days before the current date. Using this report, you can send reminders to late payers.

If you have many payments to track, a coded entry ages your accounts more reliably. In the description field of the transaction, include a code that indicates the week that payment is due (fig. 7.23). For example, you could begin the description with "W4-due" if the amount is due in the last week of January. By calling for an Accounts Receivable transaction report with W4-due in the title field of the query, you will get a report of payments due in that week and can prepare to send reminders.

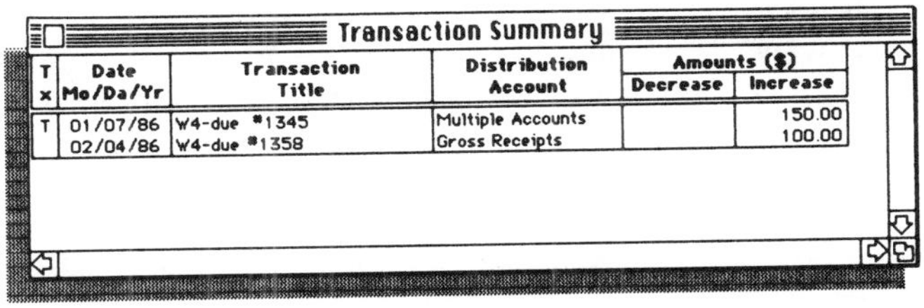
Transaction Summary
T x
Date Mo/Da/Yr
Transaction Title
Distribution Account
Amounts ($)
Decrease
Increase
T
01/07/86
02/04/86
W4-due #1345
W4-due #1358
Multiple Accounts
Gross Receipts
150.00
100.00

Fig. 7.23. A week-due code "ages" Accounts Receivable.

The same principle applies to payables. You can quickly find out what your scheduled expenditures are for any week of the year.

Client Billing for Professionals

A variation of Accounts Receivable is helpful for professionals such as dentists and analysts who have a limited number of regular clients. This method records fees, expenses, and payments while providing a way to follow up with invoices and statements.

Creating the Accounts

As an example of a professional with a small practice, a psychotherapist may have 10 regular clients. The psychotherapist can enter an ASSET Account for each client (fig. 7.24). To ensure confidentiality, the names of the Accounts are assigned codes such as CL-1, CL-2, CL-3, and so forth.

Account Definitions

In Use	Number	Account Name	Type	Monthly Budget	Starting Balance
	100	Business Checking	Check	0.00	5,000.00
	200	Acc'ts Receivable	Asset	0.00	0.00
	231	CL-1	Asset	0.00	0.00
	232	CL-2	Asset	0.00	0.00
	233	CL-3	Asset	0.00	0.00
	234	CL-4	Asset	0.00	0.00
	300	Gross Receipts	Income	0.00	
	501	Laboratory Fees	Expense	0.00	
	502	Telephone	Expense	0.00	
	503	Rent	Expense	0.00	

Fig. 7.24. Part of an Account list for a psychotherapist.

Recording Fees and Expenses

Services performed for the client are entered with Accounts Receivable as the Base Account (fig. 7.25). In this method of recording Accounts, Accounts Receivable is an ASSET. To ensure that the charges appear in the proper column, record the charges as decreases in Accounts Receivable and distribute the charges to the client's Account. As bills are paid, both Accounts Receivable and ASSET Accounts return toward a zero balance. In the transaction summary, the amount is shifted to the increase column (fig. 7.26).

Entering: Acc'ts Receivable

Base Account	Date	Description	Dist. Account	Tax	Decrease	Increase
Acc'ts Receivable	06/25	Consultation, 1hr @ $30	CL-1	T	30.00	

Fig. 7.25. A code is used to preserve the client's anonymity.

Transaction Summary

T x	Date Mo/Da/Yr	Transaction Title	Distribution Account	Amounts ($) Decrease	Increase
T	06/25/86	Consultation, 1hr @ $30	Acc'ts Receivable		30.00

Fig. 7.26. A transaction summary of the same transaction.

A lawyer often makes phone calls on behalf of a client. Any telephone expenses incurred on behalf of the client are distributed to the client rather than to the Telephone Account where the remainder of your calls are entered.

When you have already paid for a service performed for your client, record the transaction in Accounts Receivable as shown in figure 7.27.

The Laboratory Fees Account is an EXPENSE that balances the transaction. Your client is charged the laboratory fee; the fact that you already paid the fee is automatically recorded in Business Checking as a special (miscellaneous) transaction.

Fig. 7.27. Recording fees that you have paid and are billing to your client.

Editing: Acc'ts Receivable

Base Account	Date	Description	Dist. Account	Tax	Decrease	Increase
Acc'ts Receivable	08/03	Cyt. Test. Chk# 8004	-Multiple-	T	85.00	
			CL-1	T		85.00
			Business Checkina	T	85.00	
			Lab Fees	T		85.00

Submitting Bills and Statements

A compressed transaction report of your client's ASSET Account gives the information you need for bills and statements (fig. 7.28). The transaction query box lets you specify the date range which can coincide with your normal billing cycle. You could send the year-to-date summary of the report to your client by blocking out the parts of the report sheet showing figures not related to the client.

Fig. 7.28. A Transaction Summary gives the information you need for billing your clients.

Transaction Summary

T x	Date Mo/Da/Yr	Transaction Title	Distribution Account	Amounts ($) Decrease	Increase
T	06/25/86	Consultation **PAID**	Acc'ts Receivable		30.00
T	07/28/86	consult 1hr at $30	Acc'ts Receivable		30.00
T	07/30/86	consult 1 hr	Acc'ts Receivable		30.00
T	08/01/86	Paid Chk# 3333	Multiple Accounts	30.00	
	08/02/86	Phone call for CL-1	Acc'ts Receivable		10.00
T	08/02/86	Phone call for CL-1	Acc'ts Receivable		25.00
T	08/03/86	Cyt. Test. Chk# 8004	Multiple Accounts		85.00
T	08/18/86	Consult, 2 hrs @ 30	Acc'ts Receivable		60.00
T	08/28/86	Consult, 1hr @ 30	Acc'ts Receivable		30.00

Account YTD Summary

Accounts Num	Name	Type	Number Tran..	Total Amount	Current Balance
100	Business Checking	Check			
200	Acc'ts Receivable	Asset			
231	CL-1	Asset	9	270.00	270.00
402	Gross Receipts	Income			
501	Lab Fees	Expense			

Recording Payments

Accounts Receivable remains the Base Account for recording payments. Check numbers are recorded as part of the description (fig. 7.29). Distribution updates four Accounts: Accounts Receivable, Business Checking, Gross Receipts, and the client's ASSET Account. The record of the deposit in Business Checking appears as a miscellaneous transaction. A transaction report showing the client's payment can be sent as an acknowledgment of payment (fig 7.30).

Entering: Acc'ts Receivable

Base Account	Date	Description	Dist. Account	Tax	Decrease	Increase
Acc'ts Receivable	09/10	CHK # 5667, PAID IN FULL	-Multiple-	-		270.00
			Business Checking	T		270.00
			CL-1	T	270.00	
			Gross Receipts	T	270.00	

Fig. 7.29. The Accounts Receivable Account is the Base Account for recording payments.

Transaction Summary

T x	Date Mo/Da/Yr	Transaction Title	Distribution Account	Amounts ($) Decrease	Increase
T	07/28/86	consult 1hr at $30	Acc'ts Receivable		30.00
T	07/30/86	consult 1 hr	Acc'ts Receivable		30.00
T	08/02/86	Phone call for CL-1	Acc'ts Receivable		10.00
T	08/02/86	Phone call for CL-1	Acc'ts Receivable		25.00
T	08/03/86	Cyt. Test. Chk # 8004	Multiple Accounts		85.00
T	08/18/86	Consult, 2 hrs @ 30	Acc'ts Receivable		60.00
T	08/28/86	Consult, 1hr @ 30	Acc'ts Receivable		30.00
T	09/10/86	CHK # 5667, PAID IN FULL	Multiple Accounts	270.00	

Fig. 7.30. A Transaction Summary can be sent as an acknowledgment of payment.

The result of this activity is to return the client's ASSET Account to a zero balance, while updating related Accounts appropriately. At any time a year-to-date summary can tell you what any client still owes (fig. 7.31).

Account YTD Summary

Accounts Num	Name	Type	Number Tran..	Total Amount	Current Balance
100	Business Checking	Check	1	270.00	1,500.00
200	Acc'ts Receivable	Asset	1	270.00	450.00
231	CL-1	Asset	1	(270.00)	0.00
402	Gross Receipts	Income	1	270.00	2,875.[illegible]

Fig. 7.31. Year-to-date summaries always indicate a client's balance due.

A Tracking and Invoicing System for Free-Lancers

Free-lance writers, photographers, artists, craftsmen, and other professionals who market their work on speculation can use a variation of the client billing method of keeping track of where the job is and the financial arrangements for the sales. With Dollars and Sense, you can set up a simple and effective method of controlling the progress of submissions from the first mailing or delivery to invoicing and payment.

Tracking Submissions

The Dollars and Sense program can help you map the progress of your submissions. You first create an ASSET Account for every publication on your submission list (fig. 7.32). If you are submitting work to many different sources, you may wish to keep your submission records on a separate disk. On this additional disk, you also need an Accounts Receivable ASSET Account, a Gross Income INCOME Account, a CHECK Account, and EXPENSE Accounts.

Account Definitions

In Use	Number	Account Name	Type	Monthly Budget	Starting Balance
	100	Personal Checking	Check	0.00	700.00
	200	Cash	Asset	0.00	100.00
	201	People Magazine	Asset	0.00	0.00
	202	US magazine	Asset	0.00	0.00
	203	National Informer	Asset	0.00	0.00
	204	Women's Wear Daily	Asset	0.00	0.00
	205	Reader's Digest	Asset	0.00	0.00
	206	Sunset	Asset	0.00	0.00
	207	Star Weekly	Asset	0.00	0.00
	208	G.Q.	Asset	0.00	0.00
	209	Accounts Rec'ble	Asset	0.00	0.00
	300	Gross Income	Income	3,000.00	0.00
	400	Mailing	Expense	10.00	0.00
	401	Stationery	Expense	20.00	0.00
	402	Film, materials	Expense	80.00	0.00

Fig. 7.32. Account list for tracking free-lance submissions.

Record each piece of work you send off in the Accounts Receivable Account. The description field should show the title of the submission with any coding you assign to your projects (fig. 7.33). The name of the publication should appear as the Distribution Account. Until the work has been sold, leave the amount column at zero. You can also record your mailing and other costs in EXPENSE Accounts.

Base Account Accounts Rec'ble

Editing: Accounts Rec'ble **Balance: $0.00**

Base Account	Date	Description	Dist. Account	Tax	Decrease	Increase
Accounts Rec'ble	06/27	Madonna, 123	US magazine	-		0.00
Accounts Rec'ble	07/01	Miracle Drugs 124	People Magazine	-		0.00
Accounts Rec'ble	07/10	1,000-calory diet, 125	National Informer	-		0.00
Accounts Rec'ble	07/28	Dietician to Stars, 126	People Magazine	-		0.00
Accounts Rec'ble	07/30	Hollywood Hubbies, 127	National Informer	-		0.00

Fig. 7.33. Tracking stories submitted to national magazines.

Every so often, you can "age" your submissions by producing transaction reports that tell you where your work is (fig. 7.34). A follow-up telephone call may pressure a decision about using your work.

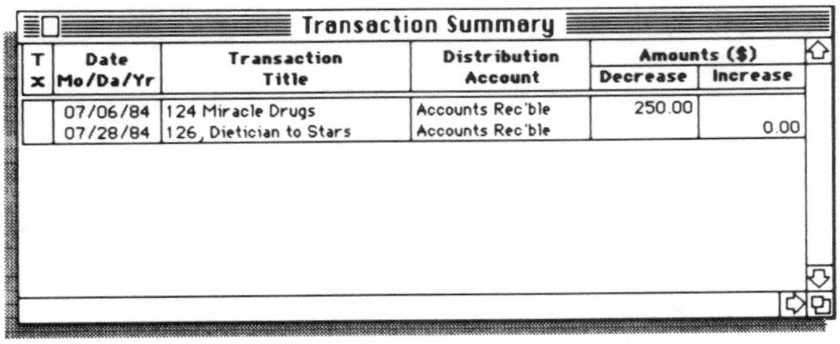

Fig. 7.34. Tracking submissions to People magazine.

After a story has been accepted, you can edit the Accounts Receivable records with the date of acceptance and the agreed fee as shown in figure 7.35. The effect of this transaction is to increase Accounts Receivable by $500 and distribute that amount to US magazine.

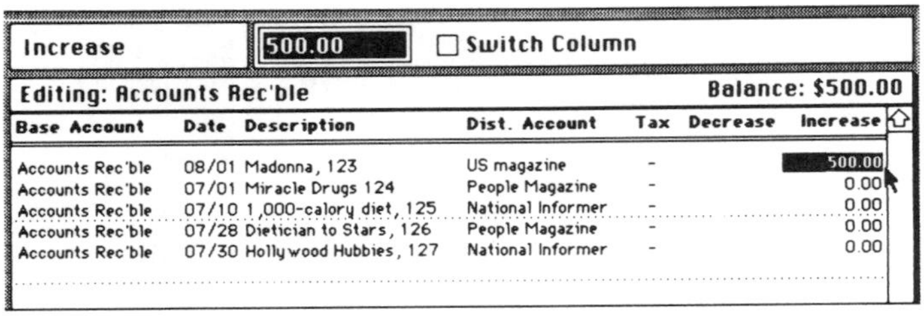

Fig. 7.35. Recording the acceptance of a story.

Making Invoices and Statements

After a story has been accepted, you can easily turn a compressed transaction report into an invoice and use the report to bill your customer (fig. 7.36).

Acceptance can also start a new aging cycle as you await payment. Set a 30-day range in your transaction reports for each publication you have entered. If you have not received payment after 30 days, you can use your transaction report as a statement of the outstanding amount.

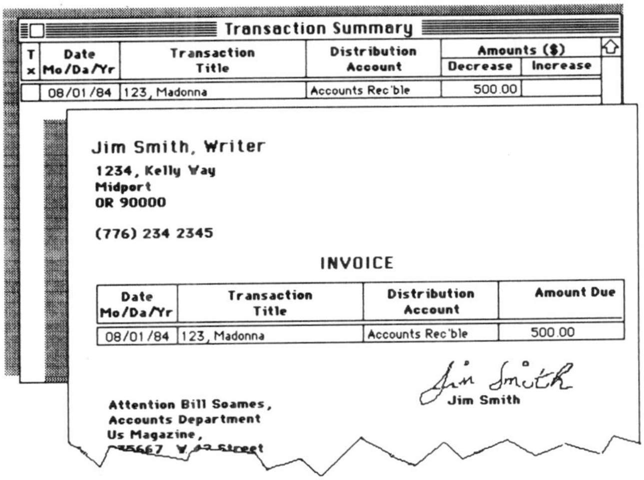

Fig. 7.36. A compressed transaction report used as an invoice.

Recording Payments

When you are paid, record the payment in your Personal or Business Checking Account as a deposit. The check number and the story identifier can be written in the description field. As shown in figure 7.37, several Accounts must be updated. The balance of your Gross Income and Personal Checking Accounts increases, while your Accounts Receivable decreases. The balance of the US Magazine Account is restored because the payment cancels out the negative amount incurred by the acceptance entry.

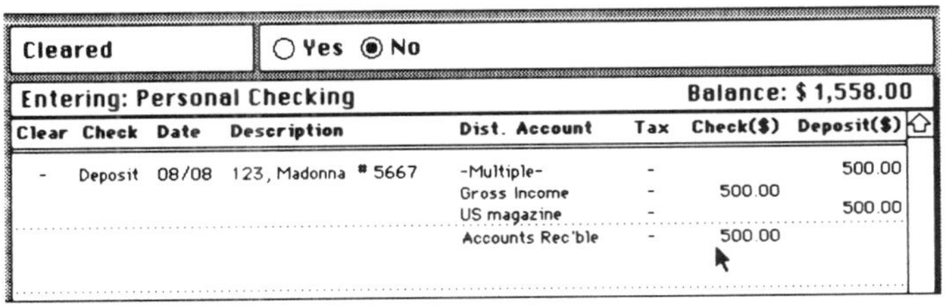

Fig. 7.37. Recording payment for a story.

Although these ASSET Accounts help track submissions, their primary function is to balance Accounts. The ASSET Accounts allow the even distribution of transactions. The balances of the Submission Accounts will always be negative when payments are due or zero if no payment is due. You can determine how much you have earned from a single source by searching for the publication's name in the title field of Personal Checking, Gross Income, or Accounts Receivable. You can also extract a transaction summary for the Publication Account and total the figures in the Increase column.

The Small Business Payroll

Electronic data processing (EDP) payroll systems have revolutionized business practice in recent years. When an established business "goes computer," payroll processing is usually the first accounting operation to be computerized.

While Dollars and Sense cannot rival EDP systems in size and scope, the program can be all a small company needs. Dollars and Sense has the power and adaptability to handle many facets of payroll preparation including record keeping, check printing, bank reconciliation, and reports to government as well as reports and graphs for company management.

Creating the Accounts

Use the Accounts in figure 7.38 for a Dollars and Sense based payroll. The difference between this arrangement and the tax-reporting needs of the individual is that taxes are liabilities for employers, not expenses.

Account Definitions

In Use	Number	Account Name	Type	Monthly Budget	Starting Balance
	100	Business Checking	Check	0.00	0.00
	300	Federal Withholding	Liability	0.00	0.00
	301	State Withholding	Liability	0.00	0.00
	302	Social Security Tax	Liability	0.00	0.00
	601	Employee Payroll	Expense	0.00	

Fig. 7.38. Creating Accounts for a Dollars and Sense payroll.

Recording the Payroll

When you write paychecks for your employees, record them in the Business Checking Account. Be sure to shift the tax amounts (fig. 7.39) so that they appear in the proper column.

Entering: Business Checking

Clear	Check	Date	Description	Dist. Account	Tax	Check($)	Deposit($)
-	2002	06/24	William James #11	-Multiple-	-	350.00	
				Employee Payroll	T		500.00
				Federal Withholding	T	50.00	
				State Withholding	T	50.00	
				Soc. Sec. Tax	T	50.00	
-	2003	06/24	Bettie Rowe #7	-Multiple-	-	400.00	
				Employee Payroll	T		565.00
				Federal Withholding	T	60.00	
				State Withholding	T	55.00	
				Soc. Sec. Tax	T	50.00	
-	2004	06/24	Anne Burns #8	-Multiple-	-	484.00	
				Employee Payroll	T		674.00
				Federal Withholding	T	105.00	
				State Withholding	T	30.00	
				Soc. Sec. Tax	T	55.00	

Fig. 7.39. The tax amounts in these payrolls have been shifted to the proper column.

Writing the Paychecks

The Write Checks option enables you to print paychecks directly from your Dollars and Sense records (fig. 7.40). After setting the number range, make sure you choose to view each check before printing. You can then add the employee's address, if you are using window envelopes, and an indication of the days or hours worked.

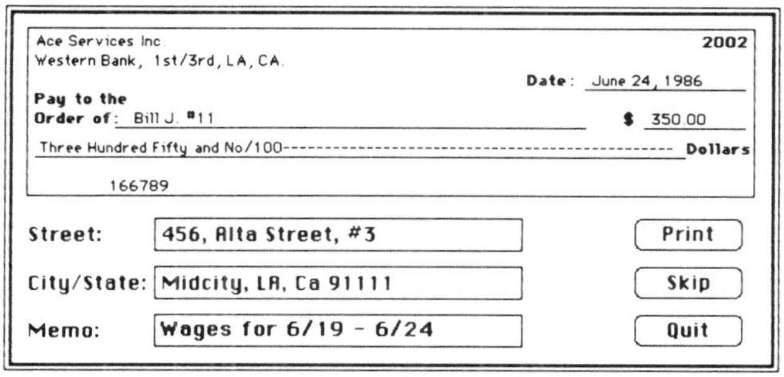

Fig. 7.40. Printing paychecks with Dollars and Sense.

Reporting Taxes Withheld

A quarterly transaction report of your Business Checking Account can tell you how much you owe various government taxing agencies (fig. 7.41).

When you pay taxes due, use the Business Checking Account again as shown in figure 7.42. Your Tax Liability Account will balance out to zero.

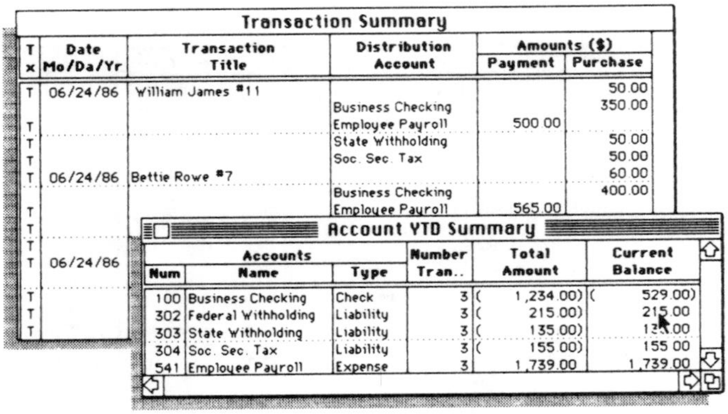
Transaction Summary
T x | Date Mo/Da/Yr | Transaction Title | Distribution Account | Amounts ($) Payment | Purchase
T 06/24/86 William James #11 50.00
Business Checking 350.00
T Employee Payroll 500.00
T State Withholding 50.00
T Soc. Sec. Tax 50.00
T 06/24/86 Bettie Rowe #7 60.00
Business Checking 400.00
T Employee Payroll 565.00
T
T
T 06/24/86
T
T
T
Account YTD Summary
Accounts Num | Name | Type | Number Tran.. | Total Amount | Current Balance
100 Business Checking Check 3 (1,234.00) (529.00)
302 Federal Withholding Liability 3 (215.00) 215.00
303 State Withholding Liability 3 (135.00)
304 Soc. Sec. Tax Liability 3 (155.00) 155.00
541 Employee Payroll Expense 3 1,739.00 1,739.00

Fig. 7.41. A transaction report showing taxes owed.

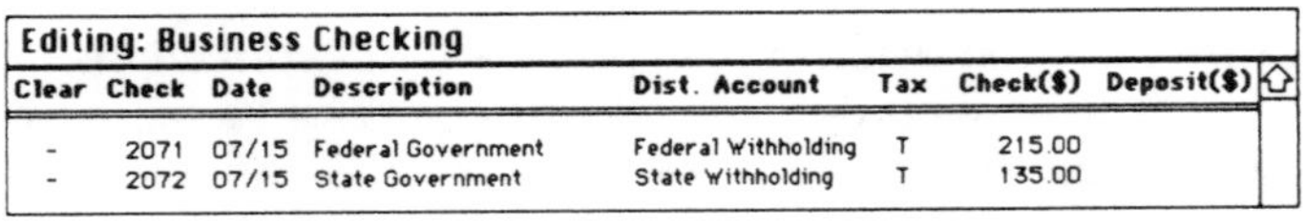
Editing: Business Checking
Clear | Check | Date | Description | Dist. Account | Tax | Check($) | Deposit($)
- 2071 07/15 Federal Government Federal Withholding T 215.00
- 2072 07/15 State Government State Withholding T 135.00

Fig. 7.42. Use the Business Checking Account to pay taxes.

At the end of the year, an annual transaction report can give the earnings statements for your employee's W-2 forms (fig. 7.43). In the transaction report query, specify the Withholding Account and use the title field to group all payments for an individual employee. If you have assigned code numbers to your employees, your grouping can be done with fewer chances of error.

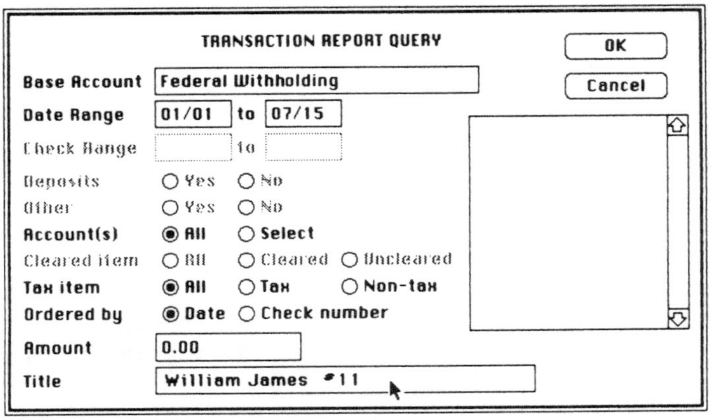
TRANSACTION REPORT QUERY
OK
Cancel
Base Account Federal Withholding
Date Range 01/01 to 07/15
Check Range to
Deposits Yes No
Other Yes No
Account(s) All Select
Cleared item All Cleared Uncleared
Tax item All Tax Non-tax
Ordered by Date Check number
Amount 0.00
Title William James #11

Fig. 7.43. Using the transaction report to obtain earnings statements.

You can use a transaction summary to show how much federal, state, and Social Security taxes were withheld from William James's paycheck (fig. 7.44).

Account YTD Summary

Accounts			Number	Total	Current
Num	Name	Type	Tran..	Amount	Balance
100	Business Checking	Check	52	(29,739.00)	11,534.80
302	Federal Withholding	Liability	52	(4,266.00	0.00
303	State Withholding	Liability	52	(750.00	0.00
304	Soc. Sec. Tax	Liability	52	(1,900.45	0.00
541	Employee Payroll	Expense	52	36,655.00	293,456.90

Fig. 7.44. The Account year-to-date summary provides information on tax withholding.

Managing Expense Accounts

Whether you are an employer, an employee, or self-employed, you can incur business expenses. Employees need to keep track of expenses for company compensation; the self-employed need to keep meticulous expense records for tax purposes. Dollars and Sense can operate as a log for recording business expenses and can give you a report of how much was spent in each category.

Creating the Accounts

In setting up the Accounts on your disk, use the guidelines of the Internal Revenue Service's list of allowable expenses. You can create a separate Account for each expense. Dollars and Sense has the added advantage of being capable of separating personal from business expenses recorded in the same Account with a title search of the T flag. Creating extra Accounts will ultimately save you work.

Your Account list should also include a Cash on Hand ASSET Account with a starting balance for handling cash payments. You should also create a LIABILITY Account for each of your credit cards and each travel and entertainment card. If you are employed, a Business Reimbursement EXPENSE Account can keep accurate records of what your employer owes you (fig. 7.45). Include a Personal Entertainment Account so that you can separate any expenditures that will not be accepted by the IRS or your boss.

Account Definitions

In Use	Number	Account Name	Type	Monthly Budget	Starting Balance
	101	Personal Checking	Check	0.00	1,000.00
	200	Business Checking	Check	0.00	500.00
	201	Cash on Hand	Asset	0.00	100.00
	306	VISA	Liability	0.00	0.00
	307	MasterCard	Liability	0.00	0.00
	308	American Express	Liability	0.00	0.00
	309	Diners'	Liability	0.00	0.00
	311	Union '76 card	Liability	0.00	0.00
	401	Business Expenses	Expense	0.00	
	403	Personal Expenses	Expense	0.00	
	404	Business Reimburse	Expense	0.00	
	406	Gas, oil	Expense	0.00	
	407	Car Repairs	Expense	0.00	
	408	Wash/ wax	Expense	0.00	
	409	Parking	Expense	0.00	
	411	Entertainment	Expense	0.00	
	412	Telephone (Bus.)	Expense	0.00	
	413	Quiet Bus. Meals	Expense	0.00	
	414	Gifts	Expense	0.00	
	416	Transportation	Expense	0.00	
	417	Lodging	Expense	0.00	
	418	Meals (out of town	Expense	0.00	
	419	Valet, laundry...	Expense	0.00	
	421	Credit card Charge	Expense	0.00	

Fig. 7.45. Accounts for managing business expenses.

As a defense for possible audits, make sure you keep all business-related receipts and a rough record of your expenses in a log book. At the same time, record transactions in the Base Account for any medium of payment, such as Cash on Hand, VISA, Checking, and so on. You do not need to access each Base Account individually because you can access them from the Accounts you use. Different Accounts are entered just by writing the Account name in the Base Account column. Figure 7.46 shows an expense record kept by an independent businessman.

Entering: American Express

Base Account	Date	Description	Dist. Account	Tax	Purchase	Payment
American Express	04/21	Lunch, Ace Pipes, Smith	Quiet Bus. Meals	T	52.00	
American Express	04/22	Acme Plant, Azusa	Gas, oil	T	22.00	
Cash on Hand	04/22	Lunch, Max's Deli	Meals (out of town	T	12.50	
American Express	04/22	Dinner with Acme Pipe	Quiet Bus. Meals	T	43.45	
Personal Checking	04/23	Desk Pen for Acme	Gifts	T	25.00	
VISA	04/23	Best Western, 1 night	Lodging	T	40.00	

Fig. 7.46. An expense record kept by an independent businessman.

To help keep accurate tax records, the independent businessman can use Dollars and Sense for entering the mileage of each business trip (fig. 7.47). This special transaction is undistributed and has no amount. At year's end, he can search for "mileage" in the title field of the transaction report query and produce complete records of business mileage.

Entering: American Express

Base Account	Date	Description	Dist. Account	Tax	Purchase	Payment
American Express	04/22	Dinner with Acme Pipe	Quiet Bus. Meals	T	43.45	
Personal Checking	04/23	Desk Pen for Acme	Gifts	T	25.00	
VISA	04/2[illegible]	[illegible]est Western, [illegible]	Lodging	T	40.00	
Personal Checking	04/[illegible]3	Azusa Mileage : 230	Undistributed	-	0.00	

Fig. 7.47. Mileage can be recorded with Dollars and Sense.

An employee can submit the report of expenses paid for company reimbursement. The complete record of out-of-pocket expenses is displayed in the Business Reimbursement Account (fig. 7.48). Partially reimbursable payments or purchases can be distributed into different Accounts (fig. 7.49).

Editing: American Express

Base Account	Date	Description	Dist. Account	Tax	Purchase	Payment
American Express	05/01	Lunch with Peak Co.	Business Reimburse	-	45.00	
American Express	05/01	Dinner with Mr Peak	Business Reimburse	-	82.00	

Fig. 7.48. The Business Reimbursement Account records business expenses.

Editing: American Express

Base Account	Date	Description	Dist. Account	Tax	Purchase	Payment
American Express	06/01	Nightclub, Peak et al	-Multiple-	-	120.00	
			Business Reimburse	-		60.00
			Entertainment	-		60.00

Fig. 7.49. A multiple distribution for partially reimbursable expenses.

Reporting Expenses

An employee claiming reimbursable expenses can submit the transaction report from that Account (fig. 7.50). Self-employed workers can use the annual reports of all business-related Expense Accounts to simplify tax returns. In addition, the reports would also be helpful to any accountant assisting in tax preparation.

When an employee is reimbursed for expenses, the check can be deposited in the employee's Personal Checking Account and distributed to Business Reimbursement (fig. 7.51). After the outstanding payments have been settled, the balance of this Account is restored to zero.

Transaction Summary

T x	Date Mo/Da/Yr	Transaction Title	Distribution Account	Amounts ($) Decrease	Increase
	05/01/86	Legal pads, stationery	Personal Checking		15.00
	05/01/86	Lunch with Peak Co.	American Express		45.00
	05/01/86	Dinner with Mr Peak	American Express		82.00
	05/02/86	Breakfast with Peak	American Express		24.00
	05/02/86	Best Western	VISA		45.00
	05/02/86	Taxi to SFX	Cash on Hand		8.50
	05/02/86	Air Fare to LAX	VISA		180.00
	05/02/86	Taxi from LAX	VISA		15.00
	06/01/86	Nightclub, Peak et al	Multiple Accounts		60.00

Account YTD Summary

Accounts Num	Name	Type	Number Tran..	Total Amount	Current Balance
101	Personal Checking	Check	1		
220	Cash on Hand	Asset	1		
306	VISA	Liability	4		
308	American Express	Liability	3		
404	Business Reimburse	Expense	9	474.50	474.50
411	Entertainment	Expense	1		

Fig. 7.50. Reports of reimbursable expenses.

Entering: Personal Checking

Clear	Check	Date	Description	Dist. Account	Tax	Check($)	Deposit($)
-	Deposit	09/07	Ch# 4456 Azusa trip	Business Reimburse	-		474.50

Fig. 7.51. Recording a reimbursement.

Suggestions for Managing Rental Property

Owners and managers of rental property are required to keep careful records of income and expenses. Whether you own one rental property or manage dozens of rentals, Dollars and Sense can perform your bookkeeping and reporting needs. Whatever the scale of your business, you should set up a separate file for your rental records including rents, security deposits, expenses, and mortgages.

Creating the Accounts

Create separate Accounts for each rental unit with sets of individual Accounts. Figure 7.52 shows a typical Account list for a two-unit rental business. Your starting balances follow the usual rules: mortgages start with the balance owed; the ASSET Accounts for the units start with their value.

The Money Market Account serves as a business checking account to record all rental transactions. You should set budgets for the INCOME

Account Definitions

In Use	Number	Account Name	Type	Monthly Budget	Starting Balance
	100	Personal Checking	Check	0.00	1,250.00
	103	Money Market	Check	0.00	200.00
	200	Cash	Asset	0.00	50.00
	202	Rental A	Asset	0.00	157,000.00
	203	Rental B	Asset	0.00	140,000.00
	231	Rental Deposits	Liability	0.00	0.00
	232	Mortgage B	Liability	54.00	90,000.00
	233	Mortgage A	Liability	67.00	107,000.00
	401	Rent A	Income	900.00	
	402	Rent B	Income	800.00	
	403	Interest Income	Income	0.00	
	590	Misc. Expenses	Expense	100.00	
	602	Repairs A	Expense	50.00	
	603	Repairs B	Expense	50.00	
	606	Mort. Interest A	Expense	0.00	
	607	Taxes A	Expense	116.66 [V]	
	615	Insurance - A	Expense	0.00	
	616	Insurance B	Expense	16.66 [V]	
	617	Insurance A	Expense	16.66 [V]	
	621	Mort. Interest B	Expense	536.00	
	622	Taxes B	Expense	100.00 [V]	
	640	Electric	Expense	50.00	
	641	Telephone	Expense	50.00	
	642	Natural Gas	Expense	50.00	
	643	Misc. Utilities	Expense	20.00	

Fig. 7.52. Creating a list of Accounts for rental units.

and EXPENSE Accounts keeping in mind that Taxes and Utilities Accounts will be variable. If tenants pay their own utilities, those expenses can be your office expenses. If the rent includes utilities, set up Utility Accounts for each unit.

Recording Rents and Deposits

Enter rent payments as deposits with Money Market as the Base Account with distribution to the INCOME Account for the rental unit. Any security deposit should be distributed to a special Account (fig. 7.53). Keep complete records of security deposits in a LIABILITY Account to ensure an accurate record of the true value of your equity.

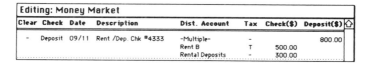

Editing: Money Market

Clear	Check	Date	Description	Dist. Account	Tax	Check($)	Deposit($)
-	Deposit	09/11	Rent /Dep. Chk #4333	-Multiple-	-		800.00
				Rent B	T	500.00	
				Rental Deposits	-	300.00	

Fig. 7.53. Recording a rent payment and a security deposit.

Paying Expenses

All major bills should be paid by check from the Money Market Account. A small business can operate on an Accounts Payable system similar to earlier models. If your business is large enough, Accounts Payable and Accounts Receivable should be kept on a separate disk with the balances transferred at the end of the month.

Your Dollars and Sense program keeps an efficient record of all expenses for balancing your books and tax reporting. A composite graph can show you at a glance which units are costing you the most in repairs and utilities.

Compiling Reports

The variety of Dollars and Sense reports can give you a picture of how your rental business is progressing. You can see a record of individual expenses in your transaction reports. Every month you should create an "operating statement" (cash flow report) that shows how your income compared with your expenses. At the end of the year an income statement can summarize your business-related expenses and income for tax reporting.

Bookkeeping for a Club or Association

Being treasurer of a club or association, such as a church group or a veterans' association, requires organization. Dollars and Sense can lighten the burden with a system for tracking the members' dues and charitable contributions.

Creating the Accounts

The association's members should be listed as INCOME Accounts. EXPENSE Accounts should be set up for different kinds of expenditures, such as film projector rental, printing and duplication, mailing, and so forth.

The following short membership list shows the monthly dues for each member as the budget for each Account (fig. 7.54). Only the CHECK Account has a starting balance, representing the money already in the bank.

Account Definitions

In Use	Number	Account Name	Type	Monthly Budget	Starting Balance
	300	William O'Dey	Income	10.00	
	301	Frank Wills	Income	10.00	
	302	Jim Snow	Income	10.00	
	303	Ernesto Blake	Income	10.00	
	304	Anatol Bondi	Income	10.00	
	100	Church Group	Check	0.00	100.00
x	998	Check Charges	Expense	0.00	
x	999	Check Interest	Income	0.00	
	400	Equip Rental	Expense	0.00	
	401	Printing	Expense	0.00	
	402	Mail	Expense	0.00	
	403	Rentals	Expense	0.00	

Fig. 7.54. Recording monthly dues for an association.

Recording Membership Dues

Membership dues are paid monthly and recorded as deposits in the CHECK Account with distribution to each member (fig. 7.55). Members who maintain their dues are reflected on the income statement as being within budget; late payers show as below budget (fig. 7.56). Transaction reports show dues paid and members' contributions, information that may be needed for tax reporting.

Editing: Church Group **Balance: $230.00**

Clear	Check	Date	Description	Dist. Account	Tax	Check($)	Deposit($)
-	Deposit	01/01	Monthly dues	Frank Wills	-		10.00
-	Deposit	01/01	Monthly Dues	Ernesto Blake	-		10.00
-	Deposit	01/01	Monthly Dues	Anatol Bondi	-		10.00
-	Deposit	01/01	Monthly Dues	Jim Snow	-		10.00
-	Deposit	01/01	Monthly Dues	William O'Dey	-		10.00
-	Deposit	02/01	Monthly Dues	Frank Wills	-		10.00
-	Deposit	02/02	Monthly Dues	Ernesto Blake	-		10.00
-	Deposit	02/02	Monthly Dues	Anatol Bondi	-		10.00
-	Deposit	02/02	Monthly Dues	William O'Dey	-		10.00
-	Deposit	03/02	Monthly Dues	Frank Wills	-		10.00
-	Deposit	03/02	Monthly Dues	Ernesto Blake	-		10.00
-	Deposit	03/02	Monthly Dues	Anatol Bondi	-		10.00
-	Deposit	03/02	Monthly Dues	William O'Dey	-		10.00

Fig. 7.55. Members names are listed in the distribution column.

Income Statement: Income

Income Accounts	First Quarter		Budget Comparison	
	Budgets	Actuals	Above	Below
William O'Dey	30.00	30.00	0.00	-
Frank Wills	30.00	30.00	0.00	-
Jim Snow	30.00	10.00	-	20.00
Ernesto Blake	30.00	30.00	0.00	-
Anatol Bondi	30.00	30.00	0.00	-
Check Interest	0.00	0.00	0.00	-
Total Income	150.00	130.00	-	20.00

Fig. 7.56. The income statement indicates which members are behind on their dues.

Raising Funds

For special fund-raising efforts, such as a church bazaar, create a new EXPENSE Account. All expenses that result from the fund-raiser are recorded in the Checking Account with distribution to the new Bazaar EXPENSE Account. All the proceeds of the fund-raiser are deposited in the Checking Account and distributed to a Fund-Raiser INCOME Account.

Managing Stocks, Bonds, and Options

Although Dollars and Sense is not designed for full-scale portfolio management, you can use the program effectively for recording and reporting your investment dealings in stocks, bonds, and options. If your holdings are small, you can integrate them with your regular Accounts lists. If your investments are substantial, and particularly if you speculate in options, records are best stored in a separate file.

Creating the Accounts

Figure 7.57 shows a typical trading Accounts list. The INCOME Accounts record your investment earnings and are separated into categories for easy tax reporting. The EXPENSE Accounts record dealer commissions and fees for other brokerage services. Most of the ASSET Accounts are for keeping records of your different types of investments. You could create Accounts for other bond holdings such as municipal bonds, series EE and HH of U.S. Treasury bonds, and so forth.

Account Definitions

In Use	Number	Account Name	Type	Monthly Budget	Starting Balance
	1	Checking Account	Check	0.00	5,000.00
	100	Money Market	Asset	0.00	50,000.00
	101	Common Stock	Asset	0.00	6,000.00
	102	Preferred Stock	Asset	0.00	2,000.00
	103	Options	Asset	0.00	0.00
	104	Bonds	Asset	0.00	14,000.00
	200	Long-Term Gains	Income	0.00	
	201	Short-Term Gains	Income	0.00	
	202	Dividends	Income	0.00	
	203	Tax-Free Dividends	Income	0.00	
	600	Broker's Comm.	Expense	0.00	
	601	Broker's Fees	Expense	0.00	
x	998	Check Charges	Expense	0.00	
x	999	Check Interest	Income	0.00	

Fig. 7.57. An Accounts list for investment records.

The file must contain at least one CHECK Account. This could be a Personal Checking Account as in the example, but you can use the Money Market Account if you use the Account only for trading.

The starting balances can be the book or face value of your stocks and bonds when you start the file. The Money Market balance represents the money you have earmarked for trading purchases.

With Money Market as the Base Account, enter a record of every new block of stock or bonds you buy. Distribute to other affected Accounts such as the appropriate ASSET and EXPENSE Accounts (fig. 7.58).

Entering: Money Market

Base Account	Date	Description	Dist. Account	Tax	Decrease	Increase
Money Market	04/14	B-2000 IBM @ 110	-Multiple-	-	220,814.50	
			Common Stock	-		220,000.00
			Broker's Comm.	-		814.50

Fig. 7.58. Recording a stock purchase.

Recording Calls and Puts

Option trading recently has become a popular investing strategy. When you ask your broker to buy a "call" on a particular stock, you do not buy the stock itself, but the right to buy the stock within a set period of time (three, six, or nine months). The option costs you a fraction of the price of the stock, and you buy the option because you believe the stock's price will rise. If the price rises, you can exercise your right to buy or sell the stock at a profit. If the price does not go up, you can try to sell the stock or take the loss—the contract price plus the broker's commission. You also can buy "puts," which work the same way except you are gambling that a stock will fall rather than rise.

Dollars and Sense is a useful tool for controlling the sometimes adventurous business of option trading. In the description field of transactions, you can include a code that warns you when the option expires: 3 for March, 10 for October, and so on.

Be sure to record confirmations from your broker in the description field (fig. 7.59). You can devise your own codes for the description field as long as you keep the codes short, or you can use the following abbreviations:

1. `B-` means that the transaction is a buy; the amount must also appear in the `Decrease` column.

2. S- indicates a sell, with the amount in the `Increase` column.
3. X is the title of the stock.
4. 55 is the strike price.

Entering: Money Market

Base Account	Date	Description	Dist. Account	Tax	Decrease	Increase
Money Market	01/10	B-10,X-3/55c @ 3.5	-Multiple-	-	3,632.92	
			Options	-		3,500.00
			Broker's Comm.	-		132.92
Money Market	02/20	S-10,X-3/55c @ 11	-Multiple-	-		10,788.33
			Options	-	3,500.00	
			Broker's Comm.	-		211.67
			Short-Term Gains	T	7,500.00	

Fig. 7.59. Recording stock transactions.

The result of the two transactions shown—a successful foray in options trading—is a handy short-term gain of $7,500. The broker's commission has been accounted for, and the Options ASSET Account has been returned to zero.

8
A Lifetime of Dollars and Sense

Dollars and Sense is a convenient, accurate money management program that is also fun to use. With this software program from Monogram, you have no need to fear either computers or money management. Available whenever you want or need to use it, Dollars and Sense can be used for your personal financial records, a small business, free-lance work, and other business applications. You require no special skills or knowledge to use the software—no need to be a computer programmer or an accountant—and you will have, literally at your fingertips, an easy to use way to keep accurate records of all your financial transactions. Accurate, convenient, and fun to use—the reports and graphs that you create with Dollars and Sense give you, whenever you want it, instant feedback of your financial situation.

If your method of keeping track of finances involves shoeboxes for receipts, a basket for bills to be paid and envelopes for those already paid, and a cubbyhole in your desk for scribbled notes about things to remember at tax time, take heart. Dollars and Sense will help you establish a certain discipline to make your life easier and your records less chaotic. After spending a little time with the program, you will find that recording transactions regularly is not difficult or painful and that the results are well worth the effort. Those who are already accustomed to managing money will find that Dollars and Sense makes the process more accurate and convenient.

You will find that the program also makes planning easy and realistic. Dollars and Sense not only shows where your money comes from and where it goes but also lets you set up a budget and compare budgeted and actual income and expenses. You can create and use graphs to see exactly how your actual income and expenses stack up against your budgets. With the program's capability for "what if?" analysis, you can dream, plan, and spend your money wisely.

Whatever the size and complexity of your business, you are sure to find Dollars and Sense useful. With this software program, you can pay bills and send invoices, write checks (yes, even payroll checks), and keep an accurate inventory. You can use the program to establish and maintain a budget and, again, to compare budgeted and actual income and expenses. With year-end information readily available, you can plot your net worth, produce reports and graphs for your own use, for meetings and, if you wish, for an annual report. Business applications are varied and easily modified to meet your specific needs.

Tax preparation does not have to be a time for heartburn and hair-pulling, thanks to Dollars and Sense. You have seen how easily you can keep track of tax-related transactions by flagging them with *T* and using the program to distribute transactions to the appropriate accounts. Pulling those T-flagged items at tax time makes filling out the tax return almost painless. And, although keeping receipts and corresponding transaction reports together will not guarantee clear sailing, should you be audited, such documentation ought to reduce confusion and might be a real help. Remember, though, that you should always treat taxes with respect and consult an expert for up-to-date information.

Monogram includes a tax-estimating and modeling program, FORECAST, with IBM versions of Dollars and Sense. This friendly program, also available for the Apple family and Macintosh, can be used with Dollars and Sense or by itself. FORECAST lets you estimate your taxes (and plan strategies) for a five-year period, and makes many important calculations automatically. You can construct any number of tax scenarios (five of them, side-by-side on screen, if you have an 80-column display) and compare, revise, store, or print them. Easily customized to suit your needs, FORECAST can also be adjusted as tax laws change.

Monogram has a careful eye on the future and is responsive to your present and future needs. Dollars and Sense may be an important chapter in the development of personal financial management, but the story is not over. You will find the program adaptable to your own constantly evolving abilities and needs. Dollars and Sense can easily be your working partner in a bright financial future.

A
Getting Started for the First Time

Starting Up and Switching Off

To start your Dollars and Sense program, place the Dollars and Sense program disk in your disk drive and switch on your computer.

If you have a Macintosh, put the program disk in the internal drive and switch the computer off and on again. Alternatively, double click on the move-to-top icon to make Dollars and Sense the start-up application.

You can stop using Dollars and Sense at any time simply by switching the computer off. If you switch off while entering data, you will lose whatever is in memory. Also keep in mind that you should not switch off when the red disk-drive light is on or when the "storing transactions" message is displayed.

Adjusting the Program To Suit Your Hardware

The initial adjustments needed to tailor your program disk to your hardware depend on which computer you have. Among the first things you see on screen will be menus for system configuration. The following are questions you may need to answer to set up your disk properly—once again depending on which computer and other equipment you have:

1. How many disk drives do you have, and which one will you use to run your system disk?
2. Will you want or need to see the screens in 40- or 80-column format?
3. Will you be using the mouse or the keyboard?
4. Will you want a list of your Accounts to be available for reference when you are entering data?
5. Which brand of printer do you have?
6. Is the program disk set up properly to work with your printer?
7. If you have a hard disk, has it been properly partitioned to accept the Dollars and Sense program?
8. Does your system have Graphics?
9. Does your system have a Hercules card?

How Many Disk Drives?

Your program is designed to be run on one or two drives or on a hard disk drive.

If you are using two drives, your program disk should be run in one drive, and your Account disk in the other. The drive in which you place your program disk to start the program is called the "boot drive." "Booting" is computer jargon for loading and starting up your program. You could call your two drives "A" and "B" or "1" and "2," but always run the program disk and the Account disk in different disk drives.

Some Apple computers need to know which disk is in which disk drive. When you boot the program in the Apple IIc for the first time, the first screen to appear asks which disk drive is to be used for the Account disk. You can change your choice of disk drives later through the Apple IIc System Configuration Menu.

40- or 80-Column Format?

The Apple IIc can show Dollars and Sense screens and reports in 40-column format. With the Apple IIc, you can switch between right and left sides of a report by pressing Control and the A key.

Mouse or Keyboard?

You can operate Apple computers with either a mouse or the keyboard. (To use the mouse, your Apple computer must have at least 128K of ram.) If you decide to use a mouse with Apple systems other than the Macintosh, you may have to switch the mouse on by using a special option of the System Configuration Menu.

Accounts List To Be Displayed While Editing Transactions?

When you are new to the program, you will probably want to keep track of the Accounts you have entered. Figuring out which Account a transaction should go into can be difficult at first. A System Configuration Menu option switches the list on and off.

Which Printer?

You do not need a printer to run Dollars and Sense, but you will find one useful. With a printer, you can print checks, make hard copies of your graphs and reports, and provide income statements for loan officers and tax accountants. Dollars and Sense has to be adjusted to work with whichever printer you have. Your choice of printers is wide and includes many name brands.

For Apple computers:

- Apple Dot Matrix
- Anadex 9501
- Epson MX-70™
- Gemini™ and EPSON
- IDS™ 445/460/560
- IDS 80/132
- NEC® 8023A/Prowriter
- OKIDATA® Microline
- TI 810/820

The Printer Type Menu is one of the first menus to appear when you start up Dollars and Sense for the first time. The menu also has another option that covers any printers not included in the lists above.

Is the Program Disk Set Up Properly for the Printer?

You can change various aspects of your printer setup with a System Configuration Menu or Print Control Menu.

If your printer is not listed on the printer type screen, you must select the "Other" option. This displays a new menu that enables you to establish some important details for your own printer.

Does the System Have Graphics?

On the System Configuration Menu, toggle *yes* or *no*.

Dollars and Sense will display graphics even if your system does not have graphics capability. Without graphics capability, however, you must respond "no" to this query for the Dollars and Sense graphics to appear.

Does the System Have a Hercules card?

On the System Configuration Menu, toggle *yes* or *no*.

When you have answered all the questions above that apply to your own hardware setup and adjusted your program accordingly, your system is "configured," and you are ready to begin using Dollars and Sense in earnest.

B
Avoiding Errors

Despite the resilience of the program, operating errors can occur for a number of reasons. Minor errors in entering data can be easily corrected, but major errors—those that destroy data—can be serious. The most common major error is damage to the disk surface by any number of things—cigarette ash, liquids, and sometimes by faulty hardware.

Reduce the chance of destroying data by protecting your disks and creating backup copies that can replace any damaged original. You can protect your disks by storing them in a dust-free paper sleeve away from moisture and extremes of heat or cold. Store your files in a rigid box to avoid crushing.

You should keep two backup copies of your Account disk at all times. Your primary backup disk should be updated after every data-entry session. A second backup should be made every week or every month, depending on how often you enter data. You should alternate the two backup copies. Update one of the copies immediately following a session, but after the next session, update the other copy. By maintaining two copies in this way, you can avoid copying an error from the original to the backup.

If a major error has occurred, all processing will stop, and an error code will appear on the screen specifying what has gone wrong. Do not back up your disk at this time because you will transfer the error to the backup disk. Instead, note the error code and, if necessary, contact Monogram for further instructions. If an error is copied onto the more current copy, you still have your weekly backup to supply data to reconstruct your work.

Monogram's Technical Support Service is available throughout the work week by calling (213) 215-0529.

Error Codes

Here are the most common error codes and what they mean.

Apple Error Codes

#16: Remove write protect tab from the program disk.

#64: Drive speed and/or alignment are not to specifications.

Solution: Make sure the monitor is not resting on the drive. Do not use a cellular phone while operating the system.

If error #64 recurs, have the drive alignment and speed readjusted to "near perfect."

Restore your records from a backup.

Macintosh Error Codes

ID= -36 The system cannot read or write onto the disk because of a problem in the external drive.

Solution: Reboot and restore. If the error persists, have the hardware checked professionally.

ID= 02 Dollars and Sense has been set to "pre-boot," as instructed by the "SetStartup" application in the finder.

Solution: Reset preboot instructions, which cannot apply to Dollars and Sense.

ID= 10 The Monogram disk is not the top item in the finder.

Solution: Double-click the "Move to Top" icon before entering Dollars and Sense.

C
Extend and Update

Extending and updating files are essential for maintaining the continuity of your financial records over the years. On your Macintosh system, `Extend` and `Update` in the File Menu initiate this activity. With other machines, the same options are available by way of the Account Disk Utilities Menu.

Extend

A Dollars and Sense file (or disk) can contain 2,000 to 4,000 transactions. When that limit or the end of the fiscal year is reached, you can start a new file as an extension of the old one.

Extending a file means carrying your Account definitions and balances over to a new file, so that disk limitations do not spoil the continuity of your records over the years. In effect, your Account set is reproduced without transactions but with budgets and starting balances equivalent to the ending balances of your old disk. The balances of EXPENSE and INCOME Accounts, however, are reset to zero, in accordance with standard accounting procedure.

For Macintosh, Extend is an option of the File Menu. Selecting Extend displays a dialog box that is a version of the Begin New File box. Check either `Extension of Year` or `Begin New Year`, and follow the instructions on the screen.

First prepare a file to receive accounts and budgets, then identify the file that contains the original definitions and budgets. You are ready to proceed with the extension.

Update

After you extend a disk, you may need to update your balances. If your bank statement comes in for reconciliation after the turn of the year, go back to your old disk and reconcile your checks. Next choose Update for the Macintosh to transfer the reconciliation balance to the new disk. Update displays two "get file" boxes, one for specifying the source of the updates, the other specifying their destination. The file that receives the updates must be an extended file.

D

The Dollars and Sense Ready-Made Accounts

Ready-Made Household Accounts

Account	*Type*	*Account*	*Type*
Personal Checking	CHECK	Clothing	EXPENSE
Cash	ASSET	Entertainment	EXPENSE
Home	ASSET	FICA	EXPENSE
Savings Account	ASSET	Groceries	EXPENSE
Stocks & Bonds	ASSET	Household	EXPENSE
Credit Cards	LIABILITY	Loan Interest	EXPENSE
Loans	LIABILITY	Medical/Dental	EXPENSE
Mortgage	LIABILITY	Misc. Expenses	EXPENSE
Check Interest	INCOME	Mortgage Interest	EXPENSE
Dividends	INCOME	Taxes-Federal	EXPENSE
Gross Income	INCOME	Taxes-Property	EXPENSE
Interest	INCOME	Taxes-State	EXPENSE
Auto Expenses	EXPENSE	Utilities	EXPENSE
Check Charges	EXPENSE		

Ready-Made Business Accounts

Account	*Type*	*Account*	*Type*
Checking Account	CHECK	Bad Debt	EXPENSE
Acc'ts. Receivable	ASSET	Check Charges	EXPENSE
Accum. Deprec.	ASSET	Cost of Goods Sold	EXPENSE
Allowance/Bad Debt	ASSET	Depreciation	EXPENSE
Buildings	ASSET	Discounts Allowed	EXPENSE
Cash on Hand	ASSET	Dues/Subscriptions	EXPENSE
Furniture/Fixtures	ASSET	Employee Benefits	EXPENSE
Goodwill	ASSET	Freight	EXPENSE
Inventory	ASSET	Insurance	EXPENSE
Investments	ASSET	Interest	EXPENSE
Land	ASSET	Legal/Accounting	EXPENSE
Machines/Equipment	ASSET	Licenses	EXPENSE
Prepaid Items	ASSET	Misc. Expenses	EXPENSE
Vehicles	ASSET	Office Supplies	EXPENSE
Acct's. Payable	LIABILITY	Payroll Taxes	EXPENSE
Mortgage/Lease	LIABILITY	Pension Plan	EXPENSE
Notes Payable	LIABILITY	Postage	EXPENSE
Taxes Payable	LIABILITY	Rent	EXPENSE
Check Interest	INCOME	Repairs/Maintenance	EXPENSE
Dividends	INCOME	Returns/Allowances	EXPENSE
Interest Earned	INCOME	Salaries/Wages	EXPENSE
Misc. Income	INCOME	Taxes	EXPENSE
Sales	INCOME	Telephone	EXPENSE
Advertising/Promo.	EXPENSE	Travel/Entertainment	EXPENSE
Auto Expenses	EXPENSE	Utilities	EXPENSE

Ready-Made Tax Preparation Accounts

Account	*Type*	*Account*	*Type*
Personal Checking	CHECK	State Tax Refund	INCOME
		Taxable Dividends	INCOME
IRA Payments	ASSET	Unemployment Comp.	INCOME
Keogh Payments	ASSET	Wages and Salaries	INCOME
Alimony Received	INCOME		
All-Savers Interest	INCOME	Accountant	EXPENSE
Cap. Gain-Long	INCOME	Advertising	EXPENSE
Cap. Gain-Short	INCOME	Alimony Paid	EXPENSE
Cap. Gain Dividend	INCOME	Auto for Property	EXPENSE
Check Interest	INCOME	Auto Registration	EXPENSE
Estates & Trusts	INCOME	Cash Contributions	EXPENSE
Insurance Reimb.	INCOME	Casualty Losses	EXPENSE
Investments/Bonds	INCOME	Check Charges	EXPENSE
Nontax. Dividends	INCOME	Credit Card Interest	EXPENSE
Partnership Income	INCOME	Depreciation	EXPENSE
Pensions/Annuity	INCOME	Doctor, dentist.	EXPENSE
Rent & Royalty	INCOME	Educational	EXPENSE
Savings Interest	INCOME	Federal Withheld	EXPENSE
Seller's Mortgage	INCOME	Insurance	EXPENSE
Interest	EXPENSE	Office Expense	EXPENSE
Interest Penalty	EXPENSE	Real Estate Tax	EXPENSE
Legal/Accounting	EXPENSE	Rent Paid	EXPENSE
Loan Interest	EXPENSE	Repairs/Maintenance	EXPENSE
Local Tax Withheld	EXPENSE	Sales Tax	EXPENSE
Medical Insurance	EXPENSE	State Withholding	EXPENSE
Medicine & Drugs	EXPENSE	Telephone/Utility	EXPENSE
Miscellaneous	EXPENSE	Travel/Entertmnt.	EXPENSE
Mortgage Interest	EXPENSE	Union Dues	EXPENSE
Noncash Contrib.	EXPENSE	Wages	EXPENSE

E
Glossary

Account—a Dollars and Sense Account is a money category that acts as a file to store transactions. Accounts can be "nominal" when representing records only, or "real" when representing actual bank accounts, liabilities, or any asset.

Account disk (or Account file)—a floppy disk that stores your Accounts and the transactions those Accounts contain.

Account definition—any of the five items of information that compose an Account: number, name, type, budget, and starting balance. Only the first three items are essential.

Account number—a three-digit number assigned to an Account, governing the order in which Accounts appear in reports and displays.

Account set—the complete list of Accounts in a file. Dollars and Sense provides three ready-made sets.

Account type—one of five Account classifications—ASSET, CHECK, EXPENSE, INCOME, and LIABILITY—that affect how the system treats Accounts.

accounting equation—Assets = Liabilities + Owners Equity (Net Worth), the basis for all double-entry bookkeeping.

accounting period—the period of time covered by an income statement: annual, quarterly, or monthly.

Accounts Payable—an Account that records amounts due to a creditor for goods and services purchased and the amounts paid for them.

Accounts Receivable—an Account that records amounts due to a debtor for goods and services sold and the amounts received for them.

actuals—the "real" amounts earned or spent. See also *budget*.

adjusted gross income—income after legally allowable deductions have been subtracted; used in calculating income tax.

appraisal—a valuation of property made by a professional appraiser.

asset—something of value that is owned, such as a car, stocks, business machinery, and so on.

ASSET Account—Dollars and Sense Account type for the things you own.

audit—the checking and verification of Accounting records.

automatic transactions—a set of transactions that are saved and can be reactivated for later use.

backup—a disk or file copied as a precaution against damage to the original.

balance—the amount in an Account, positive or negative, after all credits and debits have affected the Account.

balance sheet—a financial statement that summarizes assets, liabilities, and owner's equity at a given time.

Base Account—a major Account, often a medium of payment, used for entering transactions into Dollars and Sense. Only CHECK, ASSET, and LIABILITY Accounts can be Base Accounts. EXPENSE and INCOME Accounts can be updated only by way of a Base Account.

Note: For transaction reports, any type of Account can be used as a Base Account.

bond—a kind of promissory note issued by a company or governing body. Bonds are redeemable at face value and usually entitle the owner to interest.

boot—the act of starting up a computer or software package.

broker—someone who acts as an intermediary between persons engaged in a business transaction.

budget—the amount you expect to receive or spend in any period of time. Dollars and Sense can record both regular and variable monthly budgets.

call—a securities option purchased for a fee.

capital gain/loss—the increase or decrease in value of a capital asset. For tax reporting, gains must be split into short term and long term.

cash-flow report—a statement showing the sources of cash receipts and purposes of cash payments during an accounting period. The Dollars and Sense cash flow report analyzes cash flow for all ASSET, LIABILITY, EXPENSE, and INCOME Accounts.

CHECK—an Account type for all Checking Accounts. A Dollars and Sense Account file cannot operate unless a CHECK Account is part of the file.

check number—the number of a check transaction. The Dollars and Sense program supplies the numbers automatically but the user can override the sequence.

clear—to mark a transaction as cleared during Bank Account Reconciliation. Cleared transactions are transactions that have been processed by the bank.

closing accounts—entering transactions at the end of an accounting period to close revenue, expense, and drawing Accounts and to transfer balances to capital Accounts.

commission—a fee paid to a broker or agent for his part in resolving a transaction.

credit—a promise of future payment given in exchange for goods or services received now.

Composite Account—a set of Accounts grouped together for graphical comparisons. For example, all household expenses can be grouped in a composite Account called "House Expenses" to produce a graph showing each individual Account's share of the total expense. Your screen will hold only 12 Accounts for each graph. You could include 20 Accounts in one composite, but you would need two separate screens to see all the Accounts displayed.

current balance—the amount of money in an Account after all transactions are complete.

debit—in the double-entry system, an entry on the left side of an Account.

decrease column—the debit column of the ASSET Account entry window. Amounts are entered in ASSET Accounts as increases or decreases.

defining Accounts—the act of creating an Account in the Account definitions window.

distribution Account—any Account in which a transaction is entered indirectly by way of a Base Account.

double-entry bookkeeping—a system of bookkeeping that requires two entries in different Accounts for every transaction. The aim of double-entry bookkeeping is to keep the Accounting equation in balance.

drawing Account—an ASSET Account created to record cash drawn from a business by the owner.

Dummy Account—an Account created for the sole purpose of establishing starting balances for INCOME and EXPENSE Accounts.

editing—the process of changing transactions or Account definitions after creation.

equity—the net investment of an owner in his business.

EXPENSE—an Account type for all outlays, such as utilities, clothes, food, and so on. EXPENSE Accounts are nominal.

Expense Account—an allowance supplied by employers to employees to cover business-related expenses.

fiscal year—any 12 months selected as an Accounting period. For private individuals, the fiscal year normally coincides with the calendar year.

fixed Accounts—the Check Charges and Check Interest Accounts that are a mandatory feature of the Account list. Fixed Accounts cannot be deleted.

Gross Income Account—An INCOME Account for recording income before taxes and other expenses have been subtracted.

INCOME—An Account type for all sources of income such as Paycheck, Interest, Dividends, and so on.

income statement—a profit-and-loss statement. A report that matches income with related expenses for an accounting period. A report for calculating net income.

interest—a sum paid for the use of capital.

inventory—an itemized list of goods.

liability—a financial obligation.

LIABILITY—an Account type for your debts, such as loans, credit cards, and so on. A LIABILITY Account can be a Base Account.

menu—a list of options displayed on a computer screen. Selecting an option can begin processing.

mouse—a device for manipulating a cursor on a computer screen.

Net Annual Budget Balance—the figure that appears on the Account definition window, the product of annually budgeted income minus expenses.

net income—profit or income minus expense.

net worth—the product of assets minus liabilities.

option—an agreement to buy or sell something within a stipulated period of time.

put—an option that allows an investor to sell stock within a defined period of time.

quarter—a period of time equal to three months.

reconciliation—the process of comparing your transaction records to your bank statement and making necessary adjustments.

scroll—a technique to display a sequence of items in a list. In many cases the arrow keys can be used for scrolling through a list of Accounts.

Shift—a technique to move an amount from the debit to the credit column or from the credit to the debit column.

tax indicator—the letter *T.* During transaction entry, the indicator can mark a transaction that is tax-related (either taxable or tax-deductible).

toggle—a method of "switching" between options by pressing a key (usually a letter key).

transaction—any financial event, in particular a credit or a debit, that affects the value of an Account.

variable budget—a budget that changes from month to month.

Index

FOLD HERE

Place
Stamp
Here

Que Corporation
P. O. Box 50507
Indianapolis, IN 46250

Control Your Work Load With *Absolute Reference* And Get Your First Issue FREE!

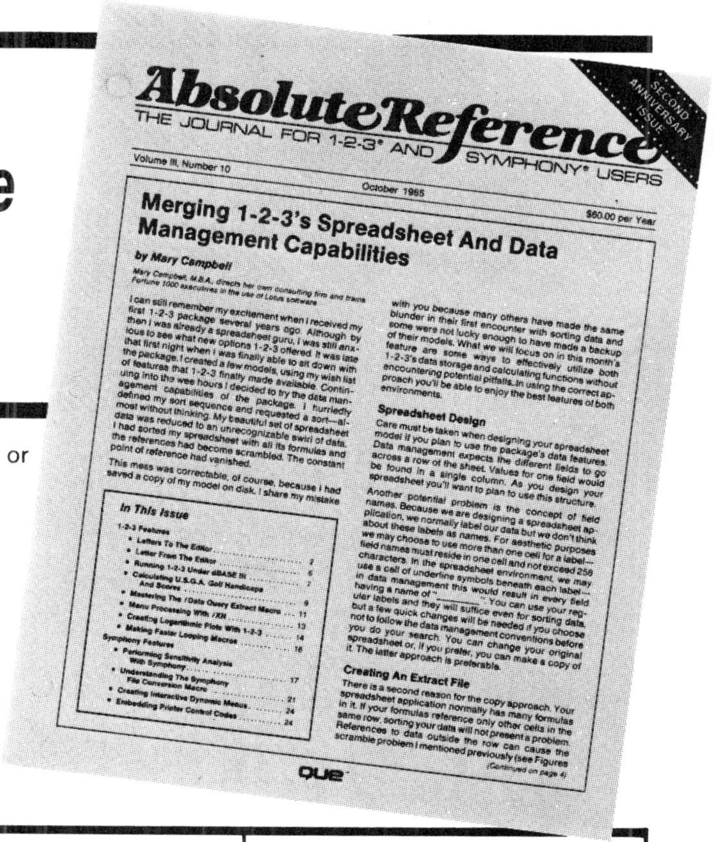

If you're spending too much time poring over 1-2-3® or Symphony® because you don't have time to develop applications, *Absolute Reference* has the answers.

For example, the monthly *Absolute Reference* can help you

- create a cash flow ledger
- compute a goal from a worksheet
- create a check writer system
- do regression analysis
- simplify investment analysis

You'll also learn from authoritative reviews which hardware works best with 1-2-3 and Symphony. And tips on the uses of various functions and commands will show you how to get the most out of your software. "Elegant" macros are a regular feature that will take the drudgery out of your work.

Find out why *Absolute Reference* is a leading 1-2-3 and Symphony productivity tool. Subscribe and get your FREE ISSUE by returning the coupon below or calling 1-800-227-7999, Ext. **500**. If this FREE FIRST ISSUE offer doesn't convince you that *Absolute Reference* is the best way to control your work load, simply write "cancel" on the invoice and return it to us. You may keep your FREE FIRST ISSUE, compliments of *Absolute Reference* and Que Corporation.

Call 1-800-227-7999, Ext. 500!

ORDER FORM

ABSOLUTE REFERENCE

Yes, I want to control my work load by subscribing to *Absolute Reference*. ($60*)

*Payable in U. S. currency. Foreign subscribers, add $20.

Method of Payment:

☐ Payment Enclosed ☐ Please Bill Me
☐ VISA ☐ MasterCard ☐ AMEX

Card # ____________________

Exp. Date ____________________

Name ____________________

Company Name ____________________

Address ____________________

City ____________________

State ____________________ ZIP ____________

QUE™ • *ABSOLUTE REFERENCE* • P. O. Box 50507 • Indianapolis, IN 46250

FOLD HERE

Place
Stamp
Here

Que Corporation
P. O. Box 50507
Indianapolis, IN 46250